THREE CENTURIES
ON THE HUDSON RIVER

One Family...One Dutch House

The story of Hoogebergh (1696-2009) and the eleven generations of the Staats family who have lived there.

W. L. Staats

Library of Congress Control Number: 2010909952 ISBN: 978-0-578-06243-3

1st Printing 2010

Printed in the United States of America

Publication editing and design by:
EHL Editorial Services
951 Myrtle Avenue Albany NY 12203-1817
518-482-6612
ileet@nycap.rr.com

DEDICATION

Among the hundreds of people who have had a positive influence on my life, there are three very special ones—in order of birth date:

Esther Staats—My resourceful, hard working, and loving mother.

Lawrence Staats—My oldest brother, who probably did more for Hoogebergh than anyone else over the centuries, thanks to his diligence and his broad areas of expertise.

Sandra Staats—My wife of 47 years, who has to have been the best daughter, wife, friend, mother, and grandmother that God ever created.

W.L. Staats

CONTENTS

Foreword   vii

Acknowledgements   ix

Introduction   1

Chapter I   Early History   3
                 The Family Name Originates in Holland   3
                 Hoogebergh and the Colonial Era   5
                 A Visit by General George Washington   7

Chapter II   The Hoogebergh Site   9
                 A Description of the Land   9
                 The Hudson River   12
                 Construction Details   16
                 A Walking Tour of the Homestead   21
                 Hoogebergh Environs   32
                 Other Dutch Homes Near Hoogebergh   38

Chapter III   The Entrepreneurial Years   42

Chapter IV   The Lean Years   47

Chapter V   The World War II Years   57

Chapter VI   The Post World War II Years Bring Dramatic Changes
                 at Hoogebergh   61
                 The Productive Years—Physical Improvements   63
                 The Lawsuit Involving an Easement   67
                 Changes in Ownership — 1982   69
                 Hoogebergh Incorporation — 1992   70
                 A Visits by the Dutch Ambassador — 1995   72

Chapter VII   Shenanigans, Annual Outings, and Celebrations   74

Chapter VIII   Remembrances from the Ninth Generation   87
                 Ghosts   87
                 Memorable Incidents   90
                 Unforgettable Personalities   95

Chapter IX   Family Lineage   119

Appendix: Recollections from Friends and Family   125

FOREWORD

A brief memoir about the Staats family, begun by William Staats, has grown into a rich book with numerous levels of interest. The text ranges from boyhood adventures to dangerous exploits from World War II, and from ancient family ties illustrated by an old cemetery on top of the hill to modern weddings. Underlying the family story is the history of the more than three centuries-old stone house in Schodack, south of Albany, New York, which has been the property of the family for 11 generations. Many houses have a story to tell, but the Joachim Staats House on Staats Island (also called Papscanee Island), tops the list. The stone house was begun in the 1690s or before and lengthened in 1722, according to a date stone. Other additions have been made, but the older parts are little changed. The text contains an invaluable record of the building updates. Hot water and electricity were late in arriving.

The first Staatses were Dutch, and the family members have remained proud of their Dutch heritage, which dates to the beginnings of New York as a Dutch colony. In the Dutch way, the family's location on the Hudson River south of Albany has always been oriented to the water. Swim across the river? Paddle across a flooded landscape in the dark? Nothing to it! Pride in their name and patrimony has kept the old house in the family's hands even during the Great Depression of the 1930s.

Author William Staats writes of his boyhood in the old stone house among a large family of brothers, and one sister, at the low point in family fortunes. He details the sacrifices which the family made before World War II to save their historic house and to keep the family intact. Since then, as times have changed, the boys have grown up, have made their marks, and family numbers have been greatly expanded. But no fear: Today a family compact assures the house will remain in Staats' hands into the future.

This is a warm story of idealistic but practical care for each other and for a house listed on the National Register of Historic Places. While the house has provided a focus for many of the descendents of Joachim Staats, the structure they have saved is a historic treasure of the upper Hudson region. This unusual book provides a fitting tribute for both the special house and the remarkable family members.

Shirley Dunn, Rensselaer County Historian
November 12, 2009

ACKNOWLEDGEMENTS

At age 77, it never occurred to me to publish a book. I had little experience in writing, history, or genealogy. In the winter of 2009, however, I visited my niece, Judy Liscum, a retired teacher who was vacationing at Daytona Beach, Florida. She had written and published three locally oriented books about St. Lawrence County in upstate New York. Judy suggested that *someone* should write a history of the Staats family in the Albany area. We are unique in that our home, Hoogebergh, was built in the 17th century and has been occupied by the same family for 313 years. I accepted the challenge.

Proofreading has been done by my daughter, Jennifer Hoeffner, and my brother, Barent Staats. A wealth of research information, encouragement, and proofreading was done by historian Shirley Dunn of East Greenbush. Niece Ingrid Solveig Staats provided several creative sketches.

Edith Leet, an experienced editor, was most helpful in correcting, suggesting, organizing, and criticizing the manuscript. Janny Venema, translator of the New Netherland Project at the State Library in Albany, New York, provided much guidance on the early history aspects of the book.

Heather Hamlin, who came in so handily with her technical capabilities in terms of advice and in creating the website.

W. L. Staats
East Greenbush, New York
March 2010

INTRODUCTION

In 1642, Major Abraham Staats (b. 1617, d. 1694), a surgeon and later a fur trader, arrived in New Netherland aboard the Dutch ship *Houttuyn*. Another passenger on that same ship was Dominie Johannes Megapolensis, who was sent over to become pastor of what is now named First Church in Albany. Abraham was the first Staats to settle in upstate New York, living in Rensselaerswyck, the patroonship of Killaen Van Rensselaer.

In addition to his surgeon profession and fur trading, Abraham was a captain on the river, commanding the sloop *Claverack*, which plied between New York and Albany.

Major Abraham Staats home in Stockport, New York, built circa 1660.

He also became involved in politics, serving as a president of the council of Rensselaerswyck from 1644 to 1648. He married Catrina Jochemse and had four sons (and perhaps a daughter) who reached maturity: Jacob, Abraham, Samuel, and Joachim. (The above information is from early Dutch records translated by Janny Venema of the New Netherland Project at the New York State Museum in Albany, NY.)

Abraham's son Joachim built Hoogebergh, a fieldstone house, beginning in 1693. Killaen Van Rensselaer, a descendent of the original patroon, deeded the property to Joachim in 1696. Since that time, Hoogebergh (Joachim's homestead) has been owned and occupied by the Staats family.

Hooge (high) Bergh (hill), translated from 17th century Dutch for "high hill," is a deliberately humorous misnomer. In earlier years, before the Staats homestead was erected, previous landholder Gysbert Cornelise Vandenbergh had lived on a high hill overlooking the Hudson on the east side and a mile or so set back from the river. When Vandenbergh relocated to the future site of the fieldstone house, which includes a 40-foot knoll located literally at the river's edge, he called the property "Hooge Berg." This knoll is far from being a high hill. (*The above information is from Shirley Dunn, "Settlement Patterns in Rensselaerwyck," de Halve Maen Magazine, 1995, p17.*)

In this book, I use the name *Hoogebergh* to refer to the house as well as to the property. Major Abraham Staats was the first ancestor to come to America and is thereby classified as the first generation of Staatses in this book. The ninth and tenth generations of Staatses are the current owners, and a healthy contingent of eleventh-generation descendents is in line to take over. The Staatses have enjoyed a rich past and present and look forward to more of the same in the future.

Personal Note: *For decades, it has been a Sunday tradition to have family members and friends (usually 15 to 20) join together for daytime relaxation preceding an early evening dinner. The bill of fare usually includes appetizers, main course, salad, green vegetables, potatoes, rolls, and dessert. Locally grown sweet corn is a special summertime treat, with apple cider as the usual beverage. No one is ever saddled with all of the work. We rotate food contribution assignments and share the preparation, serving, and cleanup. Once in a while, we take a break for an "easy" meal like subs or pizza and wings.*

CHAPTER I
EARLY HISTORY

The Family Name Originates in Holland

The following account has been framed and mounted on the wall of the master bedroom of the Staats homestead for as long as I can recall. Some have questioned its authenticity. The approximate time of this information would have been the late 1500s, when Holland was at war to gain its independence from Spain. At the present time, it is difficult to separate fact from fiction, but there seems to be a reasonable amount of truth, and it surely is interesting.

Account of the Within (Coat of) Arms,
Given with the Name of Staats

In the time of the Holland war, when they were on the point of giving up, the Grand Council of Holland being assembled to consider what method to take, one Joachim Ghyse, who was a rear admiral, gave as his opinion that he was for their becoming States.

There was at that time an account of the Spaniards expecting a flota (flotilla) from the New World (as it was then called). Holland was able to fit out five ships, which they ordered to go to a certain latitude, there to wait for the coming of the said flota, to which was one commander-in-chief, and Joachim Ghyse was second in command.

After they had been for a short time at the place the fleet was descried, and the admiral called for a council of war on board his ship, and declared that the fleet which they saw were too numerous and too large for him to encounter, and as the small fleet under his command was the forlorn hope of Holland, he would not risk an engagement, and ordered his fleet to withdraw. But Joachim Ghyse insisted that their orders were to take the flota, and he would attempt it provided any would assist him. One captain joined him in disobeying the admiral, who, with the other three, went home and complained of Ghyse' disobedience of orders.

Ghyse, with his companion, went in quest of the fleet, and out of seven took four loaded with bullion, which he escorted to Holland.

On his arrival he was fetched on shore under arrest, and brought to trial for disobeying his admiral; but on his trial produced his orders from the Grand Council, that they were to cruise for the flota and take them; on sight of which he alleged that the admiral, being a coward, was no ruler for him; as he had set out with the forlorn hope he thought as Esther, "If I perish, I perish" and he and his companion had taken four out of seven, and he believed if the admiral had remained with him the whole fleet might have been taken.

The Grand Council were so convinced of his courage and conduct that they made him admiral instead of the other (who was doomed to wear a wooden sword), and had conferred on him the surname of Staats with the enclosed arms, which by heraldists is called a speaking coat.

The Staats family coat of arms

This explained: the Crest, a Cock, denotes courage; the Helmet, being open, denotes his consequence (in relieving the Staats from ruin); the Crane on a field Argent with a stone in one claw (as that bird is said to sleep over the water and take a stone in his claws that in case he should be overcome with sleep the stone dropping into the water will wake him), the Book or Evangelist being in his beak denotes that he was earnest to preserve the faith, and the three cannon balls are emblems of his station.

This Arms, engraved on a bold gorget (an ornamental collar) with a gold chain of three thick links, he wore on a sash. (*There are still pieces of the chain in the Staats family today.*)

On the same bedroom wall where the above descriptive account is hung is a large, diamond-shaped, framed reproduction of the Staats Coat of Arms. This is not the original painting but is a reproduction that was done in the late 1800s by grandmother Jenny Ostrum Staats as she whiled away her hours at the homestead. Jenny was a city girl who preferred the bustling ambiance of New York City, where she and our paternal grandfather, Lawrence Anthony Staats, had an apartment. She detested the quiet pace of living at Hoogebergh.

Personal Note: When soliciting responses for the "Recollections" section at the end of this book, I received a most interesting letter from an old friend, Bill White, of Summit, Rhode Island. In part it read, "In 1975 Isabel (his wife) and I visited friends in Delft, Holland. While touring a cathedral there, the guide responded to my Staats question by saying, 'Ja, it's a well-known name here, sir. In fact, you are standing on one,' indicating a plaque on the floor. Later that day, we visited the archief, where we were given a two-page document, in Dutch, from a huge book of births, deaths, and marriages, which followed the family back to 1588 and the granting of a decree to Captain van Ghyse, who sailed out to help fight the Spanish Armada and lived to tell about it. The decree changed the family name to Staats. The Dutchman who bought our sailboat when we left Jakarta translated the document for us."

Hoogebergh and the Colonial Era

On April 23, 2009, I attended a presentation by the Friends of the New York State Library held at the New York State Museum in Albany. One of the speakers was Dr. Charles Gehring, director of the New Netherland Project (NNP). He discussed the Van Rensselaer family, who were one focus of the research done by the NNP. Dr. Gehring's assistant, historian and Dutch linguist Janny Venema, ably verified his comments.

According to Dr. Gehring, when the Dutch gained their independence from Spain in the late 1500s, they were governed by their Estates General. The Netherlands' outreach around the world was managed by the Dutch East India Company and the Dutch West India Company, which conducted worldwide explorations with prospects for colonization. In 1609, Henry Hudson, an English captain hired by the Dutch, sailed up the river now bearing his name to near the present city of Albany. The land was declared to be owned by the Dutch and was called the New Netherland.

To manage the colonization, the Dutch West India Company chose several patroons (colonizers), one of whom was Killaen Van Rensselaer. He was allocated two (Dutch measurement) miles on each side of the Hudson River. On the west side of the river, his allotment extended from what is now Cohoes south to approximately the town of New Baltimore. On the east side, his holdings extended from what is now Troy south to the town of Stuyvesant. The patroonship was called Rensselaerswyck.

Killaen Van Rensselaer never came to America. However, he assiduously managed Rensselaerswyck from the Netherlands by deputizing some 50 colonists to carry out his orders locally.

The Staats family is most appreciative of the efforts of East Greenbush historian Shirley Dunn, who voluntarily did the research and preparation involved in having the homestead listed in the National Register of Historic Places in 1978. Ms. Dunn has written several articles about Hoogebergh, the contents of which contain valuable and interesting information. Much of the information in the following paragraphs is taken from her article, "Settlement Patterns in Rensselaerwyck: Tracing the Hooge Berg, a Seventeenth Century Farm on the East Side of the Hudson," published in 1995 in *de Halve Maen Magazine*.

According to Ms. Dunn, Van Rensselaer purchased the Hoogebergh property from the Mohican Indians in 1637, with the purpose of establishing a few farms on the fertile land. These farms were for raising hay, cattle, and horses. In addition, along the river's shores and streambeds, the shale rock contained quartz crystals, initially thought to be valuable gems that would be of interest to Van Rensselaer, who, in addition to owning real estate, was a jewel merchant. In later years, the crystal deposits proved to be of little value.

On May 1, 1696, Van Rensselaer's descendants sold Hoogebergh to Joachim Staats, a trader, sloop owner, attorney, and politician. By that time, the fieldstone house, which had been under construction since 1693, was nearing completion. When the crown of England passed from King James II to William and Mary in 1689, Jacob Leisler fomented a rebellion in the New York colony. Joachim Staats supported the Leisler forces, but when they were quelled, he "withdrew to the stone house which he built in the 1690s."

Most of the early Dutch farmhouses were made of brick, but Hoogebergh is fieldstone. Ms. Dunn reports the speculation that the extra-thick walls of fieldstone indicate that the homestead may have been designed originally as a fort.

From Joachim Staats, Hoogebergh passed to his son, Barent, who married an Elizabeth Schuyler in 1739 and lived at the homestead. (*It was a different Elizabeth Schuyler who married Alexander Hamilton, the first Secretary of the Treasury of the new United States of America. She was the daughter of General Philip Schuyler of French and Indian War and also Revolutionary fame.*)

A sketch of "The Residence of J. P. Staats, Esq.," circa 1850.

A Visit by General George Washington

It is speculated that General George Washington, future President of the United States, spent time at Hoogebergh on June 26, 1782. According to William Spohn Baker in "Itinerary of General Washington from June 15, 1775, to December 23, 1783" (*Philadelphia: J. B. Lippincott Company, 1982*), General Washington left Newburgh for Albany on a barge on June 24, 1782, stopping along the way at posts in the vicinity.

At Albany, he was accompanied by Governor George Clinton. He was greeted by the ringing of church bells, the discharging of cannon fire, and the enthusiasm of crowds late in the day of June 26. Earlier on June 26, it is speculated that he stopped at Hoogebergh, then occupied by Lieutenant Philip Staats, who was wounded while serving in the Continental Army. Hoogebergh was only a few hours of rowing from Albany. While this visit is credible, it cannot be documented.

While at Albany on June 28, General Washington addressed the minister, elders, and deacons of the Reformed Protestant Dutch Church. On June 29, he visited the troops at Saratoga, and on June 30, he viewed the town and fortifications of Schenectady, where he was greeted by "public demonstrations and about one hundred warriors of the Oneidas and Tuscaroras, completely armed and painted for war, who met him without the gates." General Washington left Albany on July 1 and arrived back in Newburgh on July 2.

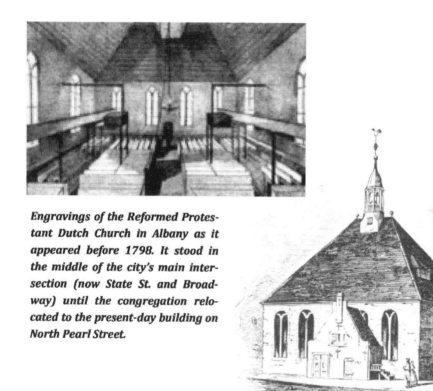

Engravings of the Reformed Protestant Dutch Church in Albany as it appeared before 1798. It stood in the middle of the city's main intersection (now State St. and Broadway) until the congregation relocated to the present-day building on North Pearl Street.

CHAPTER II
THE HOOGEBERGH SITE

A Description of the Land

Hoogebergh is located in upstate New York on the east bank of the Hudson River about halfway between Albany (the state capital) and the village of Castle-ton. The house is built some 20 feet above the river into a knoll about 40 feet high. The view south down the river from the homestead is magnificent. Large ocean-going ships as well as smaller tugs and barges ply the waters year round, along with a host of private craft during the warmer months.

In springtime, the Hudson usually floods, not only because of local precipitation but also due to the added deluge of water runoff caused by the snow melt from the Adirondack Mountains to the north. The Dutch were most foresighted, because they built the homestead at a level never reached by flooding waters. The access road (Staats Island Road) from Route 9J, however, as well as the lowland fields on the entire island are sometimes submerged under several feet of water.

Since the word "island" has been used, it should be noted that the original Staats properties included Papscanee Island, once inhabited by the Mohican tribe of Native Americans. Papscanee Island is approximately 10 miles long and one-half mile wide.

The current configuration of that body of land is an isthmus, because in the 19th century, the New York Central and Hudson River Railroad (now Amtrak) acquired an easement to the property to be used as a raised bed for its main corridor extending from Albany to New York City. At the north end of the Staats property, the creek marking the boundary of the island was filled in, while at the southern end, the creek was spanned by a railroad bridge. Thus an island was converted to an isthmus.

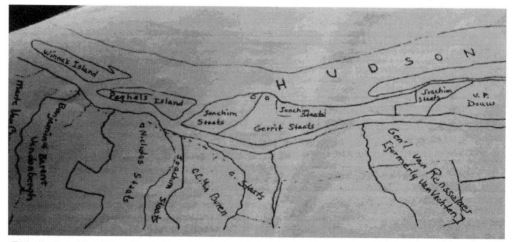

Papscanee (Staats) Island, Hoogebergh is located in the section labeled Joachim Staats. (From New York State Library, Manuscripts and Special Collections, Cherry Hill Papers, map of Papscanee, and Van Rensselaer Papers, Map 11)

Over the years, some names on the map on the next page have changed. The large island just below the word "HUDSON" is Papscanee Island, sometimes referred to as Staats Island. The island to the left of that was labeled Peghels Island on the map but was later changed to Pixtaway Island, according to Corps of Engineers' maps. The island to the far left, Winne's Island, was later named Campbell Island.

When the Hudson River channel was deepened, so much sand was pumped onto Pixtaway Island and Campbell Island that they are now one land mass. The Pixtaway land is a wetland now owned by the State of New York. A shallow creek still separates some of Pixataway Island from Papscanee Island, but river-bottom sand and a strip filled in to make the railroad bed have virtually connected Papscanee, Pixtaway, and Campbell Islands.

The railroad bed has served the important function of providing access and egress to the Staats homestead during flooding days. The bed is wide enough to accommodate two sets of rail tracks (up until the mid-20th century, when the train traffic was much heavier, there were four sets) and enough room for a vehicle. Once a determined soul braves the drive alongside the tracks far enough to reach the access to the homestead, he may still need a rowboat to bridge the expanse of water between the railroad track and the house.

Personal Note: In late winter of 1996 when the flooding was excessive, the police were alerted about an emergency situation that could have arisen for the stranded family of Barent Staats. In his 70s at the time, Barent had driven up the railroad bed and was determined to board his aluminum boat and row home. But the police interceded because they felt it was too dangerous to be rowing over freezing flood waters at nearly midnight. In the dark, Barent was able to elude the officers, stealthily hopping into his boat and vigorously managing the oars. A bystander heard the police reporting by phone that "we tried to stop him, but the old guy jumped into the boat and disappeared into the night."

In a way, the floods have been a blessing for the Staats family. To date, no developers have been interested in building on land that could be flooded several feet deep once or twice a year. With the inundation, moreover, comes a new coating of fertile silt, which makes the lowland particularly suitable for growing sweet corn, squash, pumpkins, and turnips. In recent years, an enterprising farmer has seeded considerable sod acreage.

Son-in-law Craig Hoeffner and his son, Zachary, stand on the flooded Staats Island Road in Spring 1996. The view looks east between the railroad and the highway.

Over the centuries, many of the land holdings of the Staats family have been sold, some to the railroad, some to American Oil Company, and some to others more interested in farming the land. Historically, the Staats family never were affluent, but they managed by farming, renting and selling property, and running an ice house.

By the 20th century, the land owned by the Staatses had been reduced to about 80 acres, 40 of which are bottom land on the east side of the railroad, rented out for farming, and another 40 of which are acres along the Hudson River on the west side of the tracks.

The Hudson River

Aerial view of Hoogebergh and the Staats land west of the railroad tracks.

Henry Hudson, an English explorer sailing for Holland, sailed up the river to near the site of Albany in 1609. Then called Fort Orange, the city began in 1624 as a fur-trading post. The main transportation to the outpost, some 150 miles north of New York City (then New Amsterdam), was by sloop. It must have been slow going. Up until the early 20th century, the river in the upper Hudson area of Hoogebergh was only 12 feet deep. After navigating the river to Van Wies Point, a mile or so below Albany, the sloops had to unload their passengers and cargo because a shoal prevented further progress. Choices had to be made. One option was to disembark at Staats Landing on the east bank of the Hudson, take a coach to the river ferry in Greenbush (now Rensselaer), and then cross the river to Albany. A second option was to leave the sloop at Van Wies Point and travel by coach to Albany. A popular inn, the Abbey Hotel, was available for those who embarked or disembarked the sloops at Van Wies Point. Sometimes the sloops would off-load their cargo to small boats or might even attempt to navigate the shoal at high tide.

In the early 1900s (I believe it was about 1912), the river channel was deepened from 12 feet to 30 feet. Dredges (also known as sand suckers) drew sand from the bottom of the channel and pumped it (water, sand, rocks, etc.)

through huge pipes, three feet or so in diameter, extending to the lowlands bordering the river.

Dredging operations in the Hudson River near Hoogebergh.

Since the dredging operation was conducted by the Army Corps of Engineers, channel deepening depended on Federal fund allocations. The dredginghas been carried on from time to time to the present day.

Now the channel is 40 feet deep to the port of Albany. From there north to the dam at Cohoes, the river is much shallower.

Personal Note: *For adventuresome youngsters growing up on the banks of the Hudson, the dredging process was always an inviting curiosity. I recall dredging incidents from the early 1940s. The pumps ran intermittently, and there was always a time lag of several minutes between the runs. When the pumps were in full operation, a huge blast of water, rocks, sand, etc. would rush out of the large pipes. When the pumps stopped, all was quiet. At this point in my life, I find it hard to believe that my brothers and friends and I would crawl several feet into those pipes during the quiet periods and wait for the sound of the oncoming cascade of rocks, etc. Upon hearing the threatening sound, we would scamper as fast as we could to exit the pipes just before the life-threatening force reached the outer end of the pipe. Foolhardy?...stupid?...insane? We thought it was thrilling at the time. Needless to say, our parents remained uninformed.*

In the 1930s, a popular beach known as "Little Coney Island" stretched northward along the river about a half mile north of the homestead. There was even a hot dog stand. After the war, however, the beach was filled in with rocks transported in by barge. The purpose was to prevent sand from shifting and making the river channel shallower.

Pipe three feet in diameter leading from the dredge to shore where mud, sand, rock, and water spew forth.

View south down the Hudson from Hoogebergh, summer 2009.

Personal Note: *After World War II, the river water became steadily murkier due to more commercial traffic and to the increasing pollution by cities and manufacturing corporations. In the 1950s, it wouldn't be unusual to see chunks of tar, oil streaks, and other bad stuff floating in the river. The Staats family and friends were undaunted, however. Perhaps we had developed immunities. We swam there every summer day for hours and hours. We always had a diving platform set up and a raft to swim to. Sometimes we would even ingeniously anchor a long floating log perpendicular to the docks to steer the floating debris away from the swimming area.*

In 1965, under the leadership of Governor Nelson A. Rockefeller, New York State enacted a $2 billion antipollution bill that required all municipalities and corporations dumping their waste into the river to have filtration plants. This has done wonders for the upper Hudson. The water is clearer. Vegetation that couldn't exist because of the murkiness is now growing up from the bottom. Blue crabs, which haven't been seen for decades, are present, as are the short-nosed sturgeon. The river still has a long way to go, and the recent threat of PCBs is always a scare, but progress surely has been made.

Personal Note: *For decades, it has been an annual tradition for a group to swim the 1,200-foot width of the Hudson. There are sometimes as many as a dozen bobbing heads of preteens to 70-year-olds making their way across, guarded by small boats keeping alert for river traffic and watching for anyone encountering a problem.*

Spotting Harbor Seals

Many find it incredulous that seals could be found in the upper Hudson, but several have been seen at Hoogebergh over the years. It is suspected that the seals off the coast of Long Island will follow ships up the river. Another possibility is that they follow schools of fish heading north. I have a photo from the mid-1950s of a seal reclining in the summertime on the raft near the diving area. He was later found dead from having been hit by a propeller. In 2004, another seal appeared on the ice in mid-winter. This time it was captured on camera by a local TV station.

In August of 2006, another brazen seal flipped itself up onto the rear end of our across-the-river neighbor's 15' inboard motor boat and spent the afternoon sunning itself, occasionally splashing into the Hudson to cool off. Since it was a Sunday afternoon and there was a lot of river traffic, canoeists and small-boat owners came in to see the seal. It would look lazily about, dutifully posing for photos being taken as close as 10 feet away. Again the local

TV stations had a field day. By the next morning, the seal had disappeared, never to be seen again.

Harbor seal (left of center) atop boat across the Hudson River from Hoogebergh (far right upper corner).

Construction Details

The Staats house is built on shale, and probably the house was built in two stages. There is no basement. The cellar is on the same level as the kitchen. The walls in the main section of the homestead are composed of fieldstone and mortar. Holding the walls in place are huge wooden beams, some of which are 10 or more inches square. In earlier years, we were told that the beams had come from dismantled ships that had been built from trees grown in Norway. In the recent past, however, a number of specialists in early Dutch Hudson River architecture, among them Roderick Blackburn, Don Carpentier, Paul Huey, and John Mesick, have told us that the trees came from the local area.

For some reason, the area now used as a kitchen has a ceiling supported by oak beams, while in the remainder of the original fieldstone house, the beams are pine.

The area currently used as a kitchen was once a storage area. The original Dutch-style kitchen, with its gaping fireplace, hearth, and cranes to support cooking vats, is now part of the north wing of Hoogebergh and has been incorporated as part of a modern heating system in that section of the house.

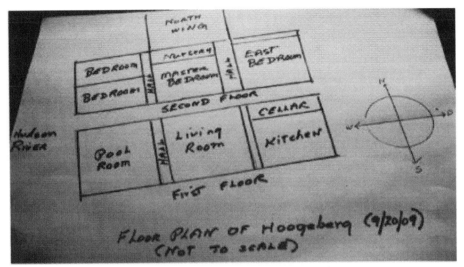

Rough sketch of Hoogebergh's floor plan

The existing roof is not the original one. Sometime in the 19th century, a fire destroyed the attic section of the house, which then was capped by a gambrel-style roof. An earlier Dutch-style steep roof probably predated the gambrel roof. The replacement roof is of standard slope. An observer can note, however, that the portion of the east outer wall of the house above the second story is made of brick. This is a very old style.

The present structure of Hoogebergh is an "L" shape with the east-west dimension being the larger segment of the "L." The north-south section is about half the size of the other dimension.

Personal Note: When I was first married and working as a school teacher and later as a college professor, I had the summer hours (when not taking courses or working part time) to spend at the homestead with my family. Over a six-year period, I decided to point up the crumbling mortar between the fieldstones. It wasn't a hard job, particularly when the effort was limited to two or three hours a morning three or four days a week. During that time, one source of frustration was the occasional "expert" who would appear in the driveway brimming with advice. The most common opinion I received was that the mortar (which I made of one part Portland cement and two parts sand) was much too solid and that over time the fieldstone would crack from the force of being crunched by too-hard cement. That remortaring job took place some 50 years ago, and the fieldstone doesn't seem to have suffered any damage.

Hoogebergh circa 1940. Note the brick at the east peak of the roof above the fieldstone first and second stories, the screened veranda, and the water tank at far right.

The house is two stories in height, and we surmise that the east end of the first floor was built and occupied while the second story was being added. A small ledge separates the two stories. The ledge appears on most old stoneand-brick houses and is intended to keep dampness from moving up the wall. Also, the ceilings of the first story are about 7.5 feet high and those of the second story are 9.5 feet.

Additions to the original structure were made sometime in the 19th century. There was an extension to the north making an "L" and a considerable extension to the west end between the original house and the river. The latter was of traditional clapboard with lath and plaster walls. In the original part of the homestead, the inner surface of the outside walls was plastered over. The outer walls of the original homestead are about 20 inches thick with an air space between the outer and inner walls of rock. This provides a cooling effect in the warmer months and preserves heat in the colder months.

The original kitchen with its Dutch fireplace in the north wing of the house.

Eighth-generation members Jenn Elliott Staats, husband Philip Staats, William Staats and wife Mary Schermerhorn Staats pose in front of the north wing porch, circa 1920.

The North Wing

While the north wing of the house is an integral part of the structure, this book will devote most descriptions to the original fieldstone house and the west wing addition. For many of the early years, the north brick wing and the fieldstone section were one unit occupied by one family. The north wing section contains the original fireplace complete with cranes for supporting heavy cooking pots and Dutch ovens for warming and baking. The north wing also has plumbing and central heating.

In the era of Lawrence Anthony Staats, the occupancy was divided so that the north wing became a separate living unit occupied by the family of his brother Philip. Extensions to the north wing were made as was the west extension to the original fieldstone homestead. After Philip died, ownership of the north wing passed to his sons, Philip and William.

The kitchen with its coal stove (center) and brick arch above the stove supporting the chimney.

After World War II, the homestead ownership was consolidated by my brothers Lawrence and Joachim. Joachim was deeded complete title to the north wing and the half acre of land on which the wing is located. In the late 1960s, Joachim sold his share of the property to brother Barent. The original fieldstone homestead and the west wing were put under corporate ownership as Hoogebergh, Inc. in 1992. By the end of 2008, 23 descendents of Esther and Lawrence Arthur Staats were shareholders. There will be more about this in a subsequent chapter.

A Walking Tour of the Homestead

It is not unusual for interested historians to find their way to Hoogebergh. If proper notice is given by telephone, the family will show a group or a few individuals through the house. Tours usually begin in the kitchen and go through the other downstairs rooms before mounting the west staircase to the second story.

Items of interest in the west wing of the house are described below.

The Kitchen

The **kitchen** is at the east end of the first story of the house. Sturdy **oak beams** support the wide-planked ceiling. Since the ceiling itself is only 7.5 feet high and the beams are 11 inches square, it was necessary for some hardworking souls to take three or more inches off the bottom side of the beams to make headroom. Imagine the skill and patience needed to pare off 3-4 inches of wood with the tools available at the time! The beams extend some 25 feet from the south to the north fieldstone walls. The cellar area was once used solely for food storage. The observer can note that the beams in the cellar are their original dimension of 11 inches square.

For **heating** the kitchen, a turn-ofthe-20th-century cast-iron wood/coal stove is used. Since the house is occupied just on weekends during the winter, only about a ton of coal is necessary for the season.

Personal Note: When I was young, a ton of soft coal was priced at about $15. That has escalated to approximately $300 in 2008.

The **cooking** is done on a modern electric range. One can carry early Dutch hardiness just so far!

Built into the kitchen ceiling and also into the living room ceiling is a **register,** a grill-like device that allows the warmer air in the downstairs rooms to rise up into the second story for winter heating of the upstairs bedrooms.

The **brick chimney** into which the stovepipe leads was replaced in the 1940s by brother Lawrence (Larry) Staats, a most capable civil engineer. Above the stove, he rebuilt the brick arch, duplicating the previous one, which was beginning to crumble. From there up to the rooftop, he built a new and safe chimney flue. In 2004, the chimney extension above the rooftop had to be remortared, and most of the bricks were replaced.

View from the kitchen window. My son Mark, 5, watches an approaching oil tanker.

The **large kitchen window** and the **walk-in pantries** were installed when the kitchen was "modernized" in the early 1920s. When my mother married and moved to Hoogebergh, there were no large windows in the kitchen because there was nothing interesting to look out at from the inside. Today's sweeping southern vista down the Hudson was blocked completely by a huge ice house, which was the family business at the time. When electric refrigeration eliminated the need for ice houses, the behemoth structure was dismantled. It was my mother's brother, Uncle Merril, who had the determination and capability to knock out part of the first-story south kitchen fieldstone wall and install a 4' x 5' "picture" window. He was also responsible for sectioning off the kitchen from the cellar by building two walk-in pantries, which are most functional.

At an earlier time, someone took the **sturdy horizontal pegs** used for hanging horse collars, etc., from the barn and mounted them along one kitchen wall. The foot-long round pegs are functional as well as serving as conversation pieces.

The west wall of the kitchen is covered by **wainscoting**.

The only **water supply** for the whole house consists of faucets above the kitchen sink. In recent years, brother Larry installed a hot water heater. Previous to that, water had to be heated on the coal stove or the electric range. The water, which is tested regularly, is pumped up to the house from a dug well about 20 feet deep. The water's purity comes from its being filtered through about 300 feet of sand. Prior to the mid-1940s, water for dishes and washing was drained by gravity system from a huge outdoor metal tank. Drinking water was hauled by the pailful and carried by hand from the dug well, which has a hand pump. In those days, drinking water was taken by dipper from a pail located on the kitchen sink.

I was told by Jim Wilbur, an elderly church colleague, that when he visited Hoogebergh in 1898, a clothes-line-type setup was used to haul water for all purposes from the then-purer waters of the Hudson River. On the premises, three different cement cisterns were used to collect rain water, which was used for all but drinking purposes.

There are no **indoor lavatories,** but two out buildings are about 100 feet from the house. One is a good-old-fashioned three-seat toilet, and the other (built in 2002) is a compost toilet. Due to its elegance (and limited capacity), the compost toilet is reserved for the ladies and for visitors.

The Living Room

The **living room** is accessed by passing through a small hallway that has stairs off to one side leading to the second story. The room, with its huge pine beams, low ceilings, and fireplace exudes an ambiance of sheer comfort.

The only source of heat in the living room is a **wood-burning fireplace** that is more than four feet wide and about three feet high. It is shallow and readily radiates heat once the fire has been roaring and the fire brick has heated. One of the sets of tongs used to stir the coals has the forge date of 1760 etched into the handle. It may even have been handled by General George Washington during his visit in 1782.

The commanding beams in the living room are 11 inches square. They were once painted a pale green to liven up the room when the ice house overshadowed and darkened the house. It must have taken several months to scrape off that paint and sand down the beams to arrive at their current natural state.

Living Room

Personal Note: It never ceases to amaze me to see pitch oozing from those centuries-old beams in wintertime when the fireplace is churning out the heat.

There is a **corner closet** on each side of the fireplace, which was once part of the west outer wall of the house facing the river.

Dutch architecture experts have told us that the two small rooms currently serving as closets were originally used for sleeping. These rooms were extremely confining, as they are only eight feet wide and four feet deep. Supposedly each of these small bedrooms had two bunks.

We have also been told that the average Dutch person at the time was about 5'1" tall and that the Dutch slept in a semi-reclining position for fear of respiratory problems if they lay prone. Even then, however, some men and women had the nickname "lange," meaning tall.

A door to one of the closets that once served as a bedroom was taken directly from a ship's cabin when the ship was dismantled. It is sloped in design, with a wedge of wood inserted at the top to make the door level. Both bedroom doors were made in the 17th century.

These little rooms have no ventilation of any kind other than the single entrance door. It must have been most uncomfortable sleeping during the winter months when windows in the living room had to remain closed, and there was so little air circulation.

On the south wall of the living room are painted **silhouettes** of three of the ninth-generation family members. These were done in the early 1940s by having the subject sit in a chair next to a kerosene lamp. The lamp created a shadow that could be penciled on the white wall and later filled in with black paint.

On the north wall of the living room hangs an **oil painting** completed in 1942 by amateur artist Frank Thomas, a neighbor who rented an apartment across the river. I was 10 years old at the time, and I can recall the entire process. I watched with fascination as the canvas was mounted on the easel and the charcoal outline was begun. It was the artist who suggested that the family should put up window shutters and paint them white to highlight the fieldstone. "And paint the living room outside door bright red so that it matches the paint on the house roof," he advised. His suggestions were heeded, which significantly enhanced the appearance of Hoogebergh.

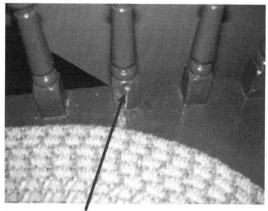

Bullet hole in stairway baluster

The Pool Room (formerly the parlor)

In the 1880s, a west wing was added to Hoogebergh. It was a good-sized extension, two stories high with a sizeable veranda on the southern and western exposures. For several years, the downstairs room was used as a sitting room or parlor. When Lawrence Arthur Staats died in 1932, his viewing was in this room. In subsequent years, a tournament-size, slatebedded billiard table was given to the family by a Castleton tavern owner in the process of closing his business. The pool room is heated by a wood stove and is often the scene of partying activities.

Personal Note: In the west wing hallway, there is a legendary bullet hole at the base of one of the balusters in the upstairs railing protecting the stairway— legendary because I had heard the story behind the incident but never had it verified. As the story goes, Arthur Staats, in his bachelor days, was playing cards with three other guys in the upstairs "blue" bedroom. An argument broke out, and Arthur accused another player of cheating. That player pulled out a pistol. Arthur ran out of the bedroom and vaulted the railing protecting the stairs in order to escape down the west wing stairway. The enraged card player aimed at Arthur and discharged a bullet, which lodged at the base of the baluster.

Hoogebergh holds many treasures. No antiques have been purchased, but a number of furnishings have become antiques over the years. Many of these are stored in the attic. A huge **map of New York State, dated 1817,** is now hanging in the pool room. On it, the Erie Canal is described as a *proposed* waterway. Native American tribes in western New York State are designated by tepees. The city of Rensselaer appears under the name of Bath, because

Rensselaer was incorporated by joining the towns of Bath, Greenbush, and East Albany after this map was made. The city of Albany is depicted by the twin towers of the First Dutch Reformed Church, the highest structure in the city at the time. This church was founded in 1642. Its present building is a brick structure built in 1798 on North Pearl Street.

Ninth-generation sailors are (l. to r.) Lawrence, Joachim, Barent, Bleecker, and William. Below are Elizabeth Jane and husband Hans Dirzuweit.

Second Story Bedrooms above the Pool Room

Upon leaving the pool room, visitors are usually invited to proceed up the stairs in the west wing, where bedrooms overlook the Hudson River, which is only a few feet away from this wing of the house. The west wing of Hoogebergh has no insulation in the walls. Anyone sleeping there on cold nights must be sure to have a few comfortable quilts for warmth.

Each bedroom is about 12 feet x 15 feet, spacious enough for bed(s), a chair, and a bureau. Each room has a wood stove, now used for decorative purposes only. Experts on antique stoves often marvel at the intricate metalwork, but it should be remembered that these stoves not only provided heat but also were an important part of the room décor in those several decades between the era of fireplaces and central heating.

On one wall of the north room, often referred to as the Blue Room, photos of the ninth generation of Staatses show all but sister Elizabeth Jane in a Navy uniform. Each of the five sons served in the Navy, three in World War II, one between wars, and the youngest in the Korean War.

The Master Bedroom and the Nursery

After leaving the twin bedrooms, visitors descend a few steps to re-enter the 1600s part of the house. The steps are necessary because the upper story of the 1880s addition was a few feet above the upper story of the original house. The master bedroom in the old section is spacious and brightly lighted by the two 5' x 4' windows with deep window seats, facing the south. The view down river is awesome.

The pine beams in the master bedroom measure 14 x 11 inches, the largest in the house. They ex-tend through this room and also the adjacent nursery, a smaller room where youngsters and fam¬ily guests often sleep. Some of the planking in the ceiling is 12 inches wide. The fireplace uses the same chimney (with a separate flue) as the one in the living room directly below.

Pine beams measuring 11" x 14" x 25' in the master bedroom.

Personal Note: *In the 1970s, I became most concerned about a myriad of tiny holes in the beams of the master bedroom. An exterminator was called in. Fortunately, this expert was more interested in the house than he was in his business, because he gave this advice: "Those holes are caused by post beetles. Judging from the limited amount of damage they have done in the past three centuries, I would suggest you should wait and contact me in another three hundred years, to see how things are." He could well have suggested the expensive process of drilling into the wood and flushing the fibers with pesticide, but he chose instead to follow the honest path.*

Personal Note: *In the 1980s, one of my teenage daughters was seeing a skilled carpenter who volunteered to remove the crumbling master bedroom plaster, re-place it with wallboard, and then paint it over. That would eliminate the bi-*

yearly chore of scraping the paint off the plaster and repainting because the cold and dampness caused the paint to peel. He did a great job. Before he could get to the nursery, however, the romance came to an end. While the daughter was searching for a new beau, I strongly suggested that she find someone who could do chimney work—to no avail.

The Upstairs Hallway

This good-sized hallway (10' x 25') has several features. A Staats family Bible, written in Dutch, rests on a stand. Notations in it of births and deaths dateback to 1704. It is interesting to peruse the family names that have been used over the centuries: Barent, Joachim, Garrett, Nicholas, Isaac, etc.

Family Bible written in Dutch (circa 1700).

Standing against one wall of the hallway is a secretary, a bureau of drawers topped by a bookcase protected by glass doors. Against another wall is a **Dutch kas,** used to store linens and blankets in the days before closets. This one has pumpkin-shaped legs, which may indicate it was brought over from Holland. Such storage closets made in the colonies by the early Dutch did not usually feature the pumpkin legs.

At the end of the hall is another set of stairs leading to a stand-up attic. The newel posts along this stairway are a product of the 17th century, we learned from one of the visiting experts on early Dutch houses.

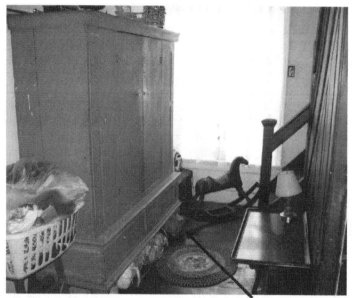

The Dutch Kas (storage cabinet). Note the pumpkin-shaped leg at the base of the kas.

When the young suitor mentioned earlier was wallboarding the master bedroom, we decided that the north/south wall of the hallway should be stripped of its plaster covering and left bare so that the original wall structure could be seen. The early Dutch had used thin tree limbs sealed with mortar composed of mud, hair, and straw. The tree limbs were held in place by vertical, hand-hewn strips of wood.

Original north/south upstairs inside wall made of limbs with mortar of mud and straw.

A skilled worker with a level would be dismayed by some of the crude workmanship of the Staats ancestors. For instance, there are two doorways in the hallway east wall. For some reason, one is two inches higher than the other.

Yet Another Bedroom---with an Adjoining Office

The final segment of the homestead tour takes the visitor to the east upstairs bedroom located across the hall from the master bedroom. In recent years, this room was occupied by brother Lawrence Staats, who died in 2008. When entering the bedroom, the visitor sees a large grotto-like opening in the west wall. This was once an upstairs fireplace supported by the brick arch in the downstairs kitchen. The fireplace bricks had crumbled and fallen, but the damage had gone undetected because this fireplace had been boarded over.

Personal Note: *Out of curiosity in the 1940s, brother Larry pulled off one of these boards and was amazed to find that the chimney had crumbled and that the wood covering it was nearly charred through by the sparks coming up from the downstairs kitchen coal stove. How blessed the family has been that a fire never resulted. That discovery prompted brother Larry to rebuild the downstairs brick arch and close in a smaller chimney flu.*

The east bedroom features what used to be a fireplace before the bricks disintegrated and fell down. This affords a good view of the old Dutch bricks (left) and the replacement chimney flue leading down to the kitchen stove on the first floor.

The beams in this bedroom are a much lighter shade of wood than the others in the house. Apparently some generations ago, a woman had a phobia about the beams falling down upon her while she slept. She persuaded her husband to construct a second ceiling under the beams. This preserved the color by protecting the beams from the elements, which included fireplace smoke.

The small room adjoining this bedroom was used as an office by brother Larry as well as by our father. The centerpiece of the office is a huge roll-top desk, complete with several drawers and several pigeon holes.

Hoogebergh Environs

A stroll around the premises reveals a number of interesting outbuildings and other landmarks.

The Cemetery

At the top of the hill is a cemetery, a commemorative site for Staats family members and their consorts. Interestingly enough, the older brownstone markers are much more legible than the white sandstone ones used later. On those sandstone markers, it is virtually impossible to read much of the inscription. Unfortunately also, some of the very old stones have cracked and the inscriptions have flaked off.

The oldest tombstone in the cemetery that is decipherable is dedicated to several family members, three of whose names Joachim (born 1654), Barrent (born 1680) and Garrets—are also the names of sons in the ninth generation (with some spelling changes). It appears to me that in the process of selecting names for their children, our mother and father consulted this stone during at least a few of her seven pregnancies.

Gravestone for Joachim Staats (1654-1712), and others.

The tallest tombstone is a memorial for Colo- nel John Graham, who died in 1794 at the age of 46. Apparently he was a veteran of the American Revolutionary War. His wife Deborah Staats Graham lived to the age of 79. Another tombstone commemorates the Joachim Staats who died in 1866. Engraved on the stone is a rooster, relating to a feature of the Coat of Arms described earlier (see page 2).

The tallest tombstone marks the graves of John & Deborah Staats Graham.

There is a stone, barely legible, for Colonel Philip Staats, who served in the Continental Army and was visited at Hoogebergh by George Washington in

1782. The Daughters of the American Revolution (DAR) have placed their commemorative emblem at this site.

Another very intriguing tombstone is a commemorative memorial to Abraham Van Alstyne, age 20 (1832-1852), the son of Abraham and Eliza Staats who died "On his passage from St. Louis to New Orleans where his remains repose." A close church friend of mine, Janet Walker, located Abraham's grave when visiting New Orleans in the 1970s.

Tombstone for Joachim Staats (died 1866).

Sometime in the early 20th century, the hilltop family cemetery was deeded to the East Greenbush Reformed Church, and that ownership status has not changed. The advantage to the Staats family is that because this is a church cemetery, additional burials can take place. As I understand it, the East Greenbush Reformed Church had transferred its cemetery to a separate foundation, but that was done before the Staats hilltop cemetery was left to that church. In the early 1990s, a representative of the East Greenbush Reformed Church contacted the Staats family to see if we would be interested in taking back possession. We declined on the basis that our cemetery, if it became private, would be subject to separate incorporation, fees, and other restrictions.

Gravestone for Col. Philip Staats, marked by the DAR's flag.

The Barn

A barn stood on the property until the early 1950s. It was a huge wooden structure with stables, a hay loft, a storage area for wood, and a deeper dug-out area that contained a hay press. The barn was torn down, and all of that area is now covered by grass, but parts of the fieldstone foundation remain as well as the dug-out area that housed the hay press. There is no trace of a nearby smaller building, which was used as a stable.

Other Outbuildings

The **outdoor toilets** are functional and kept in good repair. There are three of them: the compost toilet used by the ladies and visitors, the standard three-holer for the guys, and a separate facility for anyone located at the lower river-level area. When there are celebrations involving many attendees, we rent portable johns.

The **boat shed** was built by brother Larry in the early 1970s. Previous to its construction, canoes and other small boats were stored either on the pool room porch or in the upstairs hallway of the homestead—or they were left out in the weather!

In the 1980s, a few connected **pole barns** for storage were erected. It is amazing how an area can be filled up once a building is erected. In these structures to the south (and out of sight from the house) are most of the tools and heavy equipment. Vehicles and lawnmowers, workbenches, garage space, and boat storage facilities are all located in these protected areas.

A **carriage house** once stood on the right side of the road leading into the Hoogebergh property. It was used for storing horse-drawn vehicles. I can barely remember this structure. Today, the only evidence is a carved-out section of the hill.

The Swimming and Boating Area

In the late 1970s, Brother Larry, who had a mechanical engineering degree, took charge of building two sturdy retaining areas, one at the north end of the Staats Landing dock and one at the south end. Before anything could be started, however, thorough plans had to be submitted to and approved by the United States Army Corps of Engineers, which regulates all federal waterways, including the navigable sections of the Hudson River. Carelessly constructed projects could disintegrate and seriously hinder navigation if there was no regulation.

Personal Note: *When Larry submitted his erosion barrier construction plans to the Corps, he received a "go ahead" commendation with a complimentary phone call from one of the Corps officers. "If you can see your way clear to continuing your planned project some thirty miles south to the city of Hudson," the officer said, "the Corps would be most grateful."*

Erosion barrier crib constructed by Lawrence Staats in the late 1970s.

On the north of the Staats Landing dock and with the help of some willing assistants, Larry built a huge, triangular-shaped crib made of timbers 12" square and some 30 feet in length. This well-braced crib was then filled with truckloads of rocks.

The southern segment of the project was much more ambitious in size and scope. This involved building a huge, oblong-shaped crib with a river frontage of 20 feet and extending some 30 feet inland with a vertical height of 12 feet from the river bottom. This required the help of a crew of people, some on shore and others in rowboats, raising huge timbers to a vertical position using guidelines.

Personal Note: When the framework for the southern segment was completed, I asked how many truckloads of rocks would be needed to fill it. (We had only a cut-off Model A Ford at the time.) Larry estimated 50 or so loads. After the 130th load, the job was completed.

At that point, a commercial landscaper was hired to bring in a bulldozer to move tons of topsoil over the rock foundation. The sturdy project has held up well for more than two decades.

With the new northern erosion barrier protecting the northern extreme of the landing, it seemed an appropriate time to construct a recreation area. This consisted of a 20-foot-square deck overlooked by a grass-covered terrace of equal dimensions. The deck has proved valuable as a place to socialize under the sun, but also as a dance floor for a number of celebrations. It is almost Great Gatsby-esque to dance under the stars as the band (or DJ) holds forth on the terrace above.

Just south of the deck is a sturdy 5'-high diving platform with a fine wooden spring board. Ladders and a raft make the swimming area complete.

At the lower end of the docking area, some 30 feet of boat docking floats are attached to the dock each spring and removed in the fall to prevent ice damage. There are also a few moorings some 20 feet out in the river.

It is most sensible to have the boating and swimming areas in separate but contiguous locations.

The "Oasis" Watering Hole

As some of the women in the Staats family became less tolerant of liquid refreshments, it seemed only sensible to establish an area out of sight of Hoogebergh for late-afternoon relaxation. In 2006, a place was set up in the garage complex for just that purpose. The larger open-air portion of the garage is more spacious and comfortable in the warmer months. The inner workshop, with its closer quarters, is more ideal for cold-weather relaxation. After several options, niece Monica came up with the ideal name, "The Oasis." Friend Ben Stowell made a dandy wooden sign pointing to the location.

At the Oasis, the disorderly and confusing array of tools, equipment, working supplies, twine, and miscellaneous junk adds atmosphere. In the winter, the electric and kerosene heaters are invaluable. The mature generations often gather in the late afternoon for an hour or two of reflections and conversations that are often mundane—the weather or what was had for breakfast—and occasionally more interesting, such as politics, the stock market, news of the day, or travel plans and recollections.

Personal Note: *I recall a lingering conversation between myself, my wife, Sandy, and our lifelong friend, Wil. After several minutes of bland talk, Sandy abruptly admonished us, "You two have to be the most boring people with whom I've ever spent time. Can't you find anything interesting to talk about?" Wil, unfortunately, had in recent years become extremely hard of hearing and managed to miss Sandy's comment. He turned to me and continued our conversation, stating, "Boy, last night was a great night for sleeping!" With that, Sandy stood up and abruptly parted company.*

On another occasion, we became aware that our late-afternoon get-togethers weren't going unnoticed by the younger generation. Grandsons Matthew and Ethan were taking a high school course in consumerism. The teacher asked the class of Juniors what their plans were for retirement. One boy thought he'd like to sit around watching sports on television. A girl thought it might be a good idea to move to Florida. At this point, grandson Matthew, urged on by his cousin, raised his hand. His response to the retirement question: "I think I'd like to hang out at the Oasis like my grandfather. He really seems to be enjoying himself!"

Other Old Dutch Homes near Hoogebergh

In my early years, I can recall seeing and sometimes visiting at four other old Dutch farm homes within five miles of Hoogebergh. Much of the material below comes from *Dutch Architecture Near Albany—the Polgreen Photographs* by Shirley W. Dunn and Allison P. Bennett (1996, pp 47, 52, 77, and 84).

The **Gerrit Staats House**, built by Joachim Staats' son in 1758, was constructed just north of the knoll that separated it from Hoogebergh. It was eventually sold out of the family. In the 1930s, it was bought by Czechoslovakian immigrants Mike and Adella Podoba. They were successful, hard working, sweet corn farmers who substantially renovated the brick house because of its deteriorated condition. The Podoba family sold it, and eventually it was owned by Ray Russamano. The house burned to the ground in 1972.

The Gerrit Staats House

The **Hendrick Van Wie House**, built circa 1732, was located on the west side of the Hudson just south of Hoogebergh. To my knowledge, the house eventually fell down or burned down in the early 1950s.

Personal Note: My only recollection of the structure was in its unoccupied, dilapidated state in the late 1930s and early 1940s. For a brief time, older brother, Larry and his friends used to "haunt" the abandoned house by tying strings to make doors open mysteriously or to make bottles fall off the fireplace mantle. They might plant a friend to let out an occasional scream or groan.

They would invite their girlfriends to prowl through the house after dark, scaring the daylights out them with their antics.

The Hendrick van Wie House

I had one experience at "haunting" and that was enough. I was hiding in a darkened room awaiting the arrival of a victim whom I planned to scare, when a large creature of some kind bumped into me in the dark. I fled the scene!

The **Van Rensselaer-Genet House** located on Route 9J about a half mile north of Hayes Road, was built about 1753 and was destroyed as a potential insurance hazard in 1940.

The Van Rensselaer-Genet House

Personal Note: *To me, it was the home of cousin Pete Finkle and his wife, Mabel. Pete was renowned for his lack of ambition. I can recall him sitting by the* *fireplace and calling out, "Mabel, carry in another armload of wood; the fire's beginning to go out."*

The **Hendrick Breese House,** located immediately north of Hayes Road on Route 9J was built sometime between 1726 and 1738. It burned in 1939.

What a pity that these houses could not have stood a few more decades, when they would probably have been purchased and restored as the general public came to more and more respect the value of old Dutch architecture.

The Hendrick Breese House

CHAPTER III

THE ENTREPRENEURIAL YEARS

Lawrence Anthony Staats (1843-1921), one of nine children and of the seventh generation of Staatses, was a businessman. He and his brother, Philip, along with his maiden sister, Berthia (who did not have an ownership interest), lived at Hoogebergh. Lawrence Anthony and Philip were partners in a massive ice house, built immediately to the south of the Hoogebergh homestead. It was so overpowering in size that it dwarfed the homestead. This structure prevailed from the early 1870s until 1923, when it was torn down.

The ice house (circa 1870-1923) was huge, dwarfing Hoogebergh (to the left of the ice house). Note the barge in the river in front of the ice house.

In those years, the winters were lengthy and frigid, so much so that the Hudson River froze to a point where the ice was thick enough to be sawed into huge blocks, which were then hauled by horses into the ice house for storage.

It was hard work and involved a contingent of employees, some of whom lived in a bunk house built into the west side of the Hoogebergh knoll, about 20 feet above the river. In the warm weather months, the ice blocks were protected from melting temperatures by layers of sawdust. Huge barges would arrive at Staats Landing to transport the ice north to Albany or south to Hudson.

The Staats ice house was one of many in the area along the river. The largest was the Knickerbocker ice house on the west side of the river, just below Staats Landing.

There is scant historic information about the Staats Island ice house, which was operated by Freeman and Herick, Co. A listing found in a folder at the Albany History and Art Museum indicated that the structure held 10,000 tons of ice and measured 160 feet in length and 100 feet in width and was approximately six stories high.

Lawrence Anthony and Philip were also partners in a feed store in Greenbush, which is now the city of Rensselaer. Lawrence Anthony rented an apartment in New York City for the purpose of finding and serving customers.

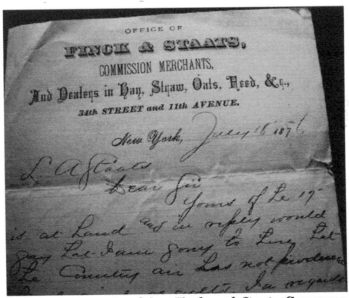

Correspondence involving Finck and Staats (Lawrence Anthony), Commission Merchants, New York City, 1871.

Philip, had two sons, Philip and William, to whom he bequeathed the north wing of Hoogebergh. These two sons also became involved in the feed store, as did Lawrence Anthony's son, Lawrence Arthur, who worked there as a clerk.

The Mohican Sailing Canoe Club

On the west side of the Hoogebergh knoll, accessible to the river, was the Mohican Canoe Club, where sailing gentlemen from the Albany area met to en joy social outings as well as sail their canoes in the summertime. This was in the early 1920s.

Mohican Canoe Club Boathouse (l.) and Clubhouse (r.), circa 1923.

Personal Note: *The club functioned during the years of Prohibition. My father used to tell of the time in his bachelor days when a group of Federal agents unexpectedly drove into the front yard of Hoogebergh, laden with axes and hammers. They ran up the hill and began smashing metal materials. When they questioned my father about the existence of a still for making liquor, he pleaded total innocence, citing that the culprits must have been accessing the still by an alternate road that approached Hoogebergh from the north side of the hill.*

This thermometer, now in the living room, was once in the Mohican Canoe Club. Note the date, 1923, and the turtle (lower center), the tribal symbol of the Mohicans.

The symbol of the Mohican Canoe Club was a turtle. In the homestead, hanging on the living room wall, is a round thermometer about a foot in diameter with the name of the club, the year 1923, and the turtle insignia on its face. In the early 2000s, when Papscanee Preserve was dedicated, members of the Mohican Native American tribe, now located in Wisconsin, were invited to attend the ceremony. The Staatses invited several to stop by at Hoogebergh for coffee. When they toured the house, the Mohicans were most pleased to see the thermometer with the turtle insignia.

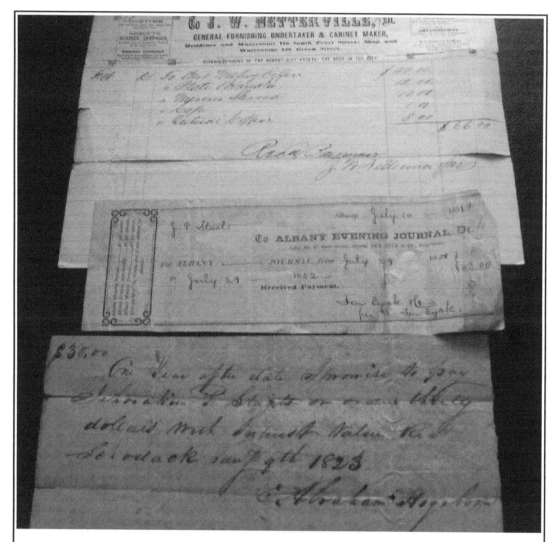

Photography was first used before the Civil War, so there are no photos of family members before Lawrence Anthony Staats. In addition, the typewriter wasn't invented until 1876, which means that earlier records were handwritten and often difficult to decipher. The penmanship in so many of the letters was beautiful with its flourishes and scrolling, but also difficult to read for those of us used to print.

The examples above, which are most difficult to read, include (*top*) an invoice to J.P. Staats from J.W. Netterville, undertaker, for a coffin, Feb 21, 1861; (*middle*) a receipt from the *Albany Evening Journal* for a subscription, July 10, 1851; and (*bottom*) a receipt for a loan of $30 from Joachim P. Staats to Abraham Hogeboom, January 9, 1823.

CHAPTER IV
THE LEAN YEARS

The Staats family was never affluent. For the first two centuries, the income from farming just about sustained the owners. In the late 1800s, the ice house at Staats Landing was a successful enterprise, but all of that came to an end when the electric refrigerator outdated the need for ice deliveries. Thus the lean years began in the early 1920s and lasted until the mid-1940s.

It was at about the beginning of the lean years that Lawrence Arthur Staats of the eighth generation took Esther Finlay Smith as his wife. He was in his late 30s at the time, fourteen years older than his bride. He worked as a bookkeeper at the family business feed store in Rensselaer. She became the mother of one daughter followed by six sons.

In their courting days, Arthur asks Esther to shoot a bottle off his head.

Personal Note: *In their courting days, Arthur (as my father was called) and Esther often took long walks on the Hoogebergh acreage. He was a great outdoorsman who was particularly active in hunting and sailing. On what was* *then called Armistice Day (now Veteran's Day), November 11, 1918, they were walking in a wooded area when her future husband asked Esther to perform a feat of marksmanship with his .22 caliber rifle. He placed a glass bottle on his head and walked several feet away and then asked her to shoot the bottle off the top of his head. She did it accurately and without hesitation. There was an act of total trust or foolhardiness —whatever!*

In 1932, at the age of 51, Lawrence Arthur fell and broke his leg. There followed a fatal blood clot, and he was gone. There was no bank account or investments, no insurance, no substantial social services—nothing for Esther Staats to support her family. She had to go on the "county dole" which was a meager welfare allocation at the time. If it hadn't been for her bachelor brother, William Ledger Smith, "Uncle Will," a railroad engineer, the family probably would have been dispersed to foster homes. This tragedy took place in 1932, right as the Great Depression was in full swing.

Neither Uncle Will nor their sister Elizabeth, "Aunt Bessie," had married. They shared a rented row house in lower Rensselaer. These two opened their hearts and their doors to their bereft sister and her six young offspring and made them a home during the weekdays so that the children could attend public school. There were only four bedrooms for the ten occupants, the largest of which (Aunt Bessie referred to it as the "dormitory") accommodated five of the six children. In spite of the lack of material things, there was a lot of love and a lot of fun—but Uncle Will and Aunt Bessie needed some breathing room on weekends.

On Friday nights the whole family would pack into the Model A Ford and drive away to Hoogebergh—as Aunt Bessie waved goodbye singing "Happy Days are Here Again."

Personal Note: In 1937, Esther bought a 1931 Model A Ford Roadster for $75 from a farm hand who had to give up driving because of alcohol problems. On Friday afternoons, after we all trooped home from school, our mother would load us into the Ford and allow her brother and sister to have some peace and quiet for two days. Aunt Bessie had one great sense of humor. She would wave goodbye to us from the front stoop while loudly singing President Franklin D. Roosevelt's campaign song at the time: "Happy Days Are Here Again" and off Mother would drive for a weekend at Hoogebergh.

Endless Toil

Throughout the 1920s and '30s, Esther Staats led a difficult life of hard work coupled with stressful challenges. The years 1931 and 1932 were the nadir. In the fall of 1931, son Garrett, age 5, was playing with matches in his bed. A fire burned him so badly that he had to be hospitalized. To get help when it happened (there was no electricity or phone at Hoogebergh in those days) on a bleak November day, Esther rowed a boat across the Hudson River and walked to the home of friends who had a phone. In spite of receiving hospital care, son Garrett contracted a fatal infection and died at home.

I was the youngest son, born William Ledger Staats on January 1, 1932. A new baby meant more and more work and worry for Esther. The second tragedy occurred in December of 1932 when her husband died as a result of a blood clot. All three of these major events took place within a 12-month period! Esther Staats, of Scots-Irish descent, determinedly made the best of her circumstances.

Esther had little time to feel sorry for herself. The household chores alone were exhausting. Washing clothes for the brood (and we always had clean, if not new, attire) was a matter of starting up a gas-powered engine that activated an ornery washing machine with a ringer that was continuously malfunctioning by getting stuck or springing open. Ironing was a chore requiring heating up hand irons on the kitchen stove. Just starting the various fires in the morning required the work of gathering kindling and larger chunks of split wood and that, of course, entailed sawing up railroad ties to burning lengths and then splitting the cut ties into stove-sized pieces.

Fortunately, most of her surviving children were old enough to help with splitting and carting wood, which was stored in the barn. The sawing of the wood was a downright dangerous task. A menacing buzz saw on a sliding platform was connected to the rear wheel of the Model A Ford by a huge belt. The car was started and put into forward gear. When the back wheel turned, it also turned the belt, which turned the axle to which the buzz saw was mounted. The railroad ties were loaded onto the platform and fed into the whirring saw. For those who participated in this scary task, the sound of the buzz saw would ring in their ears for days after the wood-cutting job had ended. The sawing of enough wood to carry through the winter was usually done over a two- or three-day weekend at Thanksgiving time.

In addition to keeping the fires going, there was endless cooking to be done. Esther never pretended to be a good cook. She much preferred flower gardening and painting woodwork. But she was excellent at certain specialties, such as doughnuts, apple fritters, and pies. As a special treat, she made bottles and bottles of sarsaparilla. Another specialty was homemade ice cream, which required hand cranking a churner for thousands of turns. There were always plenty of willing volunteers.

Buzz saw wood-cutting operation (friend Bob Currier in foreground), circa 1950.

Personal Note: *One autumn evening, brother Kim (Joachim) came home quite late. Approaching the house, he noticed a kerosene lamp burning in the kitchen. Since it was after bedtime for the family, and no one would leave a kerosene lamp lit overnight, Kim was curious. When he entered the kitchen, he was immediately "shushed" by Mother, who was sitting cross-legged on the bureau across the* *kitchen from the sink and stove area. She had a .22 rifle cradled in her arms. "I'm trying to get a shot at that rat that's been around the past few nights," she explained.*

Canning was an autumn chore. A handyman from the farm next door helped with the vegetable garden, as did her growing brood of children. She would can dozens of jars of tomatoes, corn, beans, and pickles. On the property, there were fruit trees, so canned pears and apple sauce and jam were part of the production process.

Recreation

There wasn't much time for recreation during the daylight hours with all of the work to be done. Without electricity, reading by the dim kerosene lamps was difficult. We had a battery-operated radio. Listening to Sunday evening radio shows (Fred Allen, Jack Benny, Edgar Bergen and Charlie McCarthy) was a favorite family pastime.

The Hendrick Hudson Day Liner, built in 1906 with a capacity of 5,300 passengers, passes by Hoogebergh.

Hoogebergh was ideal for outdoor fun. In the summer, the young family spent a good portion of the daytime **swimming**. We would also catch minnows left high and dry by waves generated by passing tugs and ships. The gracious fleet of the Hudson River Day Line passed by twice daily, one ship going south to New York City at mid-morning, and a different one heading north toward Albany in late afternoon. These awesome ships usually had side-paddle-wheel propulsion and three or four decks for passengers. The Hendrick Hudson could accommodate a few thousand. On board, the wide staircases had mahogany railings. Potted plants were used for decoration, and a small music combo often played. A favorite food available was the "Lillian Russell"—half a cantaloupe with a scoop of vanilla ice cream resting in the middle.

Because we lived on the banks of the Hudson, **boating** played an integral part in our lives. At age 17, Brother Kim salvaged a huge metal lifeboat from one of the day liner passenger ships. He fashioned a well for an outboard motor at the rear keel of the boat and also built a crude cabin. While it never moved very fast, it was adequate for overnight camping trips, carrying Kim and the older brothers and friends several miles down river from Hoogebergh.

Brother Larry in his homemade rowboat, (circa) 1939.

Personal Note: *During the summer after his high school graduation, brother Lawrence and four of his buddies embarked on a daring adventure. Even in his teens, his engineering talent was put to the test when he constructed his own 15' rowboat. On the transom, he mounted an outboard motor. Using this vessel, five teenagers set off on a five-day excursion 150 miles south to New York City. They endured problems with a faulty carburetor, rain storms, and choppy waters, but* *they made it. One night they slept in Central Park, and they took the opportunity to visit Times Square and eat at an Automat, where prepared sandwiches were available in a glass case once you slipped the proper number of coins into the slot. Some of the guys attended a major league baseball game. They returned home full of exciting stories. One of the fellows was so afraid his Mom would have a fit that he never told her about it as long as she lived.*

A unique form of summer entertainment involved **climbing and bending poplar** trees. There were literally hundreds of these young trees poking up through the sand that had been pumped out of the river channel when the Hudson was deepened.

Brother Bleecker stands by as younger brother Bill dangles helplessly.

If the trees were about four inches in diameter at the base, they were very flexible. One had only to climb the limbs upward and eventually the tree would bend over and enable the climber to get a ride downward until he reached the sandy soil below. Most of the time!

Personal Note: I recall when, as an eight-year old, I was goaded to climb a poplar by older brother Bleecker (now there's a Dutch name for you). This particular tree was unusually high, and when I climbed as far up as was possible, it began to bend —and then it stopped. This stranded me some 12 feet off the ground, and the tree bent no further. "Help me!" I cried plaintively to my older brother.

Bleecker patiently waited at the base of the tree. Then there was a crack, the tree broke, and I came plummeting down with a thud as I hit the sand. "Why didn't you help me?" I beseeched him. His reply: "No need for that. I knew you'd be down—eventually!"

Croquet has been a family favorite for decades. I recall a game in the 1940s when two elderly ladies were on competing teams, and one of them cheated by nudging her ball with her foot. As youngsters, croquet was a favorite pastime involving both siblings and neighbors. Brother Bleek was the agitator. It seemed to the rest of us that his only goal for playing was to send the competition far beyond boundaries (and in those days we didn't have a rule about being able to return to the boundary line.)

On one occasion, brother Barry threatened to strike Bleek with his mallet. On another, I literally chased brother Bleek across the course with my mallet raised and poised for striking. Fortunately for him, brother Bleek was a faster runner. I was assured by an onlooker, however, that had I launched the mallet, it would have struck its intended target: Bleek's head!

In the 1990s and early 2000s, several members and friends of the Staats family entered into croquet competitions held on the grounds of Clermont, the Robert Livingston estate. Pairs of competitors usually come from the local area, and many are seasoned competitors. The Staats contingent has often won the tournament. As recently as the summer of 2008, grandson Zachary and his dad, Craig Hoeffner, took the competition title.

When large groups gather in the summer, **softball, volleyball, bocce, or horseshoe pitching** are often the afternoon entertainment.

In the wintertime, there was **ice skating** on the small ponds and (when safe) the frozen river. Before the 1940s, the channel wasn't kept open for commercial river traffic. The ice would sometimes freeze to a thickness of a foot or more during the extremely cold winters. It wasn't unusual to walk across the river to visit friends and, for safety's sake, one often carried a long pole suspended horizontally to catch on either side of an ice hole in case one's leg went through. If someone did fall though, there was the imminent danger of being carried under the ice by the current.

Nephew Charles "Chip" Staats takes aim with his croquet mallet.

Ice boat racing was a fun time for my older brothers and their friends. It had its dangerous aspects, however, because of the excessive speed and the possibility of being injured by a metal runner.

Tobogganing and sledding were usually an option, because Hoogebergh is built on a 40-foot knoll that slopes significantly down to the river. Those who were sledding would start at the cemetery and enjoy several hundred feet of sledding down the south side of the hill before coasting to a stop somewhere near the well-water pump. For the brave, there was the option of sledding or tobogganing down the steeper eastern slope of the hill that led to a cornfield— or the west slope of the hill, which took one right out on the frozen river. That hazardous option was seldom taken.

Yet Another Tragedy

On November 4, 1939, a group of the Staats brothers were gathered around an outdoor campfire near their homemade clubhouse complex several hundred feet south of the house on the old ice house foundation. For some reason, I was facing away from the fire when the wind took a dramatic change in direction. Without my knowing it, my sweatshirt caught on fire. Once I realized the impending disaster, I ran as rapidly as possible toward the river, several hundred feet away. By this time, my clothing was ablaze. An older brother tackled me, but by that time considerable burning had taken its toll.

I was wrapped in a blanket and whisked off to what was then called Albany City Hospital, where I was consigned to the burn unit. I was lucky to survive the severe burning, which did the most serious damage to my neck and underarms. For some four months, I stayed in the hospital receiving treatments of gentian violet, the burn cure at the time. When the healing was finished, a web of scar tissue connected my chin to my chest. The same type of scar tissue prevented me from raising my arms above shoulder level.

During the hospital stay, at a time when visiting hours were only on Wednesday afternoons and weekends, Esther Staats seldom missed a visiting date. She was there by my side throughout the ordeal.

It was most fortunate that the hospital had on its staff a Doctor Harold Browne, who'd taken an interest in plastic surgery in the days before it became a specialized procedure. He persuaded Esther to let him, at no cost, experiment with replacing scar tissue with transplanted skin from other parts of my body, mainly my legs. This involved some half dozen operations over a period of five years, and it worked! It cost me one year of schooling. I had to repeat the third grade because of time lost. My third grade teacher regularly visited the hospital to cheer up her injured student.

CHAPTER V
THE WORLD WAR II YEARS

In a previous paragraph, I mentioned the family's routine of listening to late Sunday afternoon and evening radio shows. One family favorite was a scary mystery program called "The Inner Sanctum" with a host named "Raymond." It had some very thrilling episodes and was most popular. We would blow out the kerosene lamps and listen in darkness to add to the spookiness.

What happened on one such Sunday evening was way beyond scary. It became one of those unforgettable events in my life like the assassination of President John F. Kennedy and the attack on the World Trade Center. It was December 7, 1941, and family and friends were glued to the radio listening to the eerie program with its "creaking door" when one of brother Larry's friends, Howard Lout, burst through the living room door with a devastating announcement: "This morning Pearl Harbor in Hawaii was bombed by the Japanese," he reported. "President Roosevelt has declared war on Japan!"

Shock was the universal reaction. Many in the room were in their late teens. A few months later, several of them had joined the armed services.

Brother Kim and Howard Lout were the only ones who were directly involved in the conflict, while brothers Barent and Lawrence and their other friends served during the war but didn't see any "action." Howard Lout was seriously injured in the battle of Corregidor.

Personal Note: Brother Kim had no taste for high school. On his way to school on December 8, he tossed his lunch into a ditch and headed directly to the Navy recruiting office. His first assignment was aboard a Destroyer Escort (DE), but he became so seasick that he was advised to either leave the Navy or serve aboard a submarine. He chose the latter. In the years after the war, Kim rarely talked about his experiences in the war theater. It was only in his 70s that he came forth with some shocking stories of his adventures aboard the submarine USS Whale.

Kim's experience that I remember best was the daring attempt of the submarine's rescue efforts to save a pilot whose plane had crashed into the lagoon of an island occupied by the Japanese. In the dead of night, the Whale *stealthily propelled into the bay, which was protected by explosive mines suspended in the water. A sailor was seated on each wing of the tail fin, and his job was to gently kick the mines out of the way as the sub progressed. Brother Kim was in the sleeping quarters and could hear the mines softly bumping against the outer hull of the* Whale. *The experience was so stressful that the sailors on the fins were replaced every half hour. With a great deal of good fortune, the submarine was unharmed, and the rescue effort was a success!*

World War II submarine USS Whale *on which brother Joachim (Kim) served.*

There was a great deal of patriotism during World War II. Red and white flags with blue stars denoting the number of offspring in the military were proudly displayed in living room windows. Upon meeting on the street, anxious parents would hug other parents, and tears flowed freely. The talk centered entirely on the war. Many items were rationed, including sugar, coffee, gasoline, shoes, and tobacco.

A World War II ration book and stamps issued to uncle William Smith by the Office of Price Administration (OPA).

Bond rallies involved big-time entertainers such as Kate Smith, Bing Crosby, and the Andrews Sisters. We had practice sessions involving blackouts, when every light in the house had to be extinguished. Sometimes the local volunteer fire marshal would show up at the door to ensure no lights were aglow. America was following the lead of the British who endured endless air raids. War movies and newsreel segments were the features in most theaters.

At Hoogebergh, life was subdued. Most of the young men were in the service. The highlight was when they came home for a respite. Without helping hands to do the chores, the house took on a seedy look, with dangling shutters and wood- work sorely in need of paint.

Esther labored on, caring for those too young to serve. Uncle Will saw to it that sister Jane attended business school. My fondest memories of my sister, the eldest of the siblings, involved her playing the piano in the living room at the homestead during the 1930s and '40s. She would buy her sheet music at Kresge's (now Kmart) five-and-dime store on North Pearl Street in Albany. Every Sunday, she would carry an armload of sheet music back and forth to the homestead. We often sang around the piano Sunday evenings in those years.

Sister Jane married one of brother Larry's closest friends just before the war ended. Brother Kim was only 20 when in 1943 he married his sweetheart, Kay, who lived across the river from the homestead.

Hoogebergh fell into disrepair during World War II.

CHAPTER VI

THE POST-WWII YEARS BRING DRAMATIC CHANGES AT HOOGEBERGH

It was a joyful time when the older Staats servicemen and their buddies returned from tours of duty. Fortunately, none had suffered a serious disability, although brother Kim had a severe hearing impairment from the constant racket of the submarine engines.

At this stage of their lives, physical capabilities and mental attitudes had changed for many veterans. There was a burst of enthusiasm that was electrifying, and it spilled over to Hoogebergh.

Since the early 1900s, Hoogebergh had been under the joint ownership of four eighth generation Staatses. Two of them were cousins Philip Staats and his brother, William, who owned and operated the feed store where my father, Lawrence Staats, worked as a bookkeeper.

When Phil died, he left his share of Hoogebergh to his widow, cousin Jen. When cousin Will died, his share went to his daughter, Elizabeth. The other two owners of Hoogebergh were my father, Lawrence Staats ("Arthur"), and his sister, Mabel Staats Higgins, from whom Arthur was estranged. When Arthur died, he left his share to his widow, Esther.

Personal Note: Every family has skeletons in the closet. With cousin Will Staats, the rumor is that he was in a fatal auto accident in the early 1900s and that the last person he asked for before dying was his paramour and not his wife. The other story involved Mabel Staats Higgins. It seems that on her honeymoon in winter visiting Niagara Falls, she pulled her hand out of the hand muff and a note slipped out and fell to the ground, whereupon her new husband picked it up and read it. The note was a recently written love note to Mabel's paramour. Even in those days there were "juicy" stories!

The ownership by the seventh and eighth generations had remained relatively static over the decades from the 1860s until the 1940s. In the 1920s, all except my father wanted to sell Hoogebergh. Because he exercised his veto power, the sale never took place. The other owners took little interest in the homestead, and it gradually fell into disrepair. If my father had agreed to sell, Hoogebergh would have gone out of the Staats family, which at that time had owned and occupied the homestead for some 225 years.

Following their discharges from the service, brothers Larry and Kim agreed to look into buying out the ownership of cousin Phil's widow and cousin Will's daughter. The two ladies were approached. Cousin Jennie Elliott Staats, Phil's widow, who was a lovely old lady in her 80s, practically gave her share to the boys. Elizabeth Staats Schell, who inherited her father Will's estate, turned negotiation over to her husband, and months of bargaining ensued until a selling price agreement was reached.

A most interesting enigma occurred with the attempt to locate Aunt Mabel Staats Higgins, whose last known whereabouts was in Newburgh, New York, some 90 miles south of Albany. There had been no contact with her in decades. When Larry and Kim finally located her address, they found that she had recently died destitute as a ward of the county. They were able to settle with an attorney who was designated by the county to handle the estates of indigent people.

After the purchase, Larry and Kim (Joachim) each owned one-half of Hoogebergh. Kim was to have complete ownership of the north wing and an additional one-half ownership of the main fieldstone structure. This wasn't crystal clear in the negotiated settlement, and for decades it was thought that Kim owned only the north wing. Larry, who owned half of the old house and the west wing, divided his share equally among himself; his mother, Esther Staats; and his four siblings: Elizabeth Jane, Barent, Bleecker, and William. This ownership status held firm until the early 1980s.

As stated earlier, there was little in terms of financial resources in the family. No one yet had a college education, and all worked hard at their employment. Any improvements to Hoogebergh had to be done by family members with limited resources—but improvements there were, and some were dramatic.

Electricity

Even though electricity was available, it wasn't introduced to Hoogebergh until 1946. Lawrence Staats, "Arthur," of the eighth generation, had been told that in order to get electric wiring to the homestead, some three-fourths of a mile from the main highway, he would have to pay for the utility poles, wiring, and labor to get it to the house. The cost was prohibitive.

In 1946, brother Kim learned that the county owned most of the access road to the homestead and that the county would have to pay for the poles. The only cost to the family would be for setting those poles and for electrical service on our private property. The cost became manageable.

Electrical service set the tone for amazing changes at Hoogebergh. Both Larry and Kim were experts at installing the wiring, and in a matter of months, the homestead had been considerably modernized. Kerosene lamps were replaced by much brighter electric ones. Electric radios, irons, ranges, refrigerators, vacuum cleaners—the works!—along with enough electrical outlets in every room. It was practically paradise!

Running Water to the Kitchen and to the North Wing

Brother Kim hired an indigent laborer to dig a ditch connecting the dug fresh-water well to the defunct cistern to the south of the house. Another trench was dug from the cistern to the house. Then he installed a pump in the cistern and installed the plumbing necessary to have a cold-water faucet in the kitchen and a pipe leading to the north wing, where he had a hot-water heater and a full-fledged plumbing system. No more would it be necessary to hand-carry water from the well to the house.

All these changes were done by the labor of Larry and Kim. We couldn't have those things without them, because we just couldn't afford the cost to have them done by outside contractors.

The Productive Years — Physical Improvements

In the mid-1940s, after brothers Larry, Kim, and Barry were discharged, brother Bleecker joined the Navy. For most of his time in the Navy, he was stationed on Guam.

Personal Note: Prior to joining the service, brother Bleecker had become interested in photography. At about that time, colored slides came into vogue. He took many, many—too many—photos while stationed on Guam. When he came home from there, he would show the Guam slides over and over and over. One observer said, "It seems he showed the Guam slides every time it got dark." A relative who had a restless child would bring her to the door and ask Bleek to show the Guam slides—and the child would doze off into dreamland.

After Bleek completed his Navy tenure, he joined the Coast Guard and was assigned to a station in New York Harbor with subsistence and quarters in Jersey City.

I joined the Navy at the time of the Korean War, serving on active duty from 1952 to 1954.

Brother Kim and his wife decided to move to a more modern home in the village of Nassau back in the early 1960s. For several years after that, he rented out the north wing to a succession of tenants.

Family Losses:

Esther Staats, Arthur's widow and the hard-working matriarch of Hoogebergh, died in December of 1966 after being struck by an automobile while crossing a busy street.

Sister Elizabeth Jane died suddenly from an aneurism while she was standing on the altar making an announcement in church. The year was 1977, and she was only 57.

Brother Bleek contracted prostate cancer and died at the age of 65 in 1994. Brother Kim died from cancer at the age of 78 in 2003.

Brother Larry battled colon cancer and also congestive heart failure, which finally took him in 2008.

Hoogebergh Improvements

Once the family had reached full maturity—gainfully employed and bursting with ambition—Hoogebergh prospered from their efforts to physically improve the premises. Over the decades since the 1950s, literally dozens of improvements to the property have been made. A complete list would be impossible to compile, since many of the accomplishments were not as thoroughly documented as those done by brother Larry.

Personal Note: *Lawrence Staats was a typical engineer: thorough and organized. Whenever he started on a project, he would write down its objective and draw an open circle next to the notation. At the various stages of working on the project, he would color in the circle. A circle half filled in indicated that he was half finished with the job. He also kept track of his financial outlays. Larry's journal has proved to be of increasing importance as a reference since his death. For instance, there have recently been problems with the fresh-water pumping system. Consulting Larry's journal has enabled those of us attempting to solve the problem to see sketches and read a detailed description of the water system.*

Improvements to Hoogebergh included:

- Continuous improvement of the electrical service. Service was increased to 220 volts, 200 amps, and was extended to the toilets, the boat shed, and the garages in 1971. It was further extended to the river-front area in 1992.
- Replacing the kitchen floor, including new foundation beams and heavy-duty plywood covered with high-grade linoleum (1970-71).
- Remortaring the fieldstone on the south and east walls of the original homestead (summers beginning in 1969 and ending in 1976).
- Rebuilding the north wall, which had practically crumbled due to weather damage.
- Rebuilding the chimney from the kitchen to the rooftop.
- Replacing the roofing and reshingling with cedar shakes the three porches attached to the house (1977-78).

Personal Note: *At age 4, grandson Zachary of the eleventh generation was dropped off with his grandfather, who agreed to baby sit. Zachary was commandeered to help with reroofing the poolroom veranda. For safety measures, grandfather tied a lightweight rope to the waist of his young helper so that he couldn't fall off the roof. The rope, which was tied on a firm hook, was long enough to allow Zachary to help out by putting the old nails in a coffee can. The boy thoroughly enjoyed the job. Not so his mother who, upon returning to Hoogebergh and seeing her young son up on the roof, nearly fainted.*

- Rebuilding the diving platform—three times (1955, 1972, 2006).
- Constructing two erosion barriers along the riverfront (1977, 1983-84).
- Constructing a riverfront deck (1983) and later replacing it with a higher deck (1998-99). The terrace overlooking the deck was created in 1984.
- Building a sturdy boat shed for a storage area for canoes and a sailboat and for a workshop (1967-69).
- Building five sets of connected pole barns for storage areas (1983, 1985-86, 1998).
- Building a second set of pole barns for boat storage (1985-87).
- Constructing a 10'-square stone patio in front of the kitchen entrance (1990).
- Creating several mini-parks by clearing brush and seeding lawns in areas that were previously woodlands among scrub and weeds

(1984 88). In addition, we increased the lawn area from about two acre to four acres, giving Hoogebergh a more enhanced setting. Prior to the 1960s, the only maintained areas were the flower garden on the south of the house and about an acre of lawn on the east side. From 1950 through 2008 additional lawn areas were added.

- Building low fencing along the Hudson riverbank south of the homestead. This fencing extends about 500 feet and serves as a retainer to prevent floating debris from washing in and covering the lawns in times of flooding (2005).
- Renovating the "office" adjoining the east bedroom by pointing up crumbling mortar, covering walls with wallboard, installing new baseboards, and painting (2000).
- Creating a putting green (2007).

Personal Note: Brother Barent is responsible for the mini-parks, fencing, and improved river-viewing areas. He also had a professional come in to level and develop a golf putting green, even though he never held a golf club in his life. Apparently his motive was to please those who had developed an interest in golf.

- Creating a system for pumping water up from the Hudson and installing faucets in six different locations near the homestead, the north wing, the lower garages, and near the river bank (1991).
- Covering the dirt floor in the cellar with a three-inch layer of concrete (1991).
- Constructing an outdoor shower, complete with hot-water service, for warm weather showering (2008).
- Reconstructing the section of the kitchen chimney extending above the roof of the house and pointing up the living room chimney (2005).
- Installing newly sanded and painted white shutters on second story windows in the fieldstone section of the house (1982).
- Constructing an Adirondack-style lean-to, built by a town of Red Hook Boy Scout troop led by brother Bleecker (1976).
- Replacing rotted window sills in the upstairs bedrooms (1977-78).
- Putting a new copper roof over the western extension (1998). This was done by contractors in a rare concession to the need for outside expertise. Previously, a tarpaper roof that needed annual upkeep to stop leaking was kept in shape by brother Barent.

- Constructing two open pole barns to serve as wood storage sheds (1985).
- Constructing a spacious gazebo on the terrace overlooking the river (2008-09).
- Adding a hot-water shower to the changing-room section of the compost toilet (2009).

The gazebo completed in the spring of 2009.

In addition to the above projects at Hoogebergh, the continual tasks of mowing, gardening, painting, raking, cleaning, machine repairing, and so on are all done by family and friends in an endless effort to keep Hoogebergh in good condition.

Every four years (the year of the presidential election), there is the formidable task of painting the tin roof that covers the original section and the north wing of Hoogebergh. If this is delayed for more than four years, the tin begins to rust, which requires scraping before painting. In earlier years, painting was done with a broad paintbrush, but in recent years, a paint roller has proved to be more efficient and quicker. In 2004, a pressure washer was first used to remove the loose paint and dirt before the hand painting is started. No matter which way you slice it, it's a big job involving several days of physical effort.

The Lawsuit Involving an Easement

In 1965, a building boom of enormous proportions began in the capital city of Albany. It was generated by construction of a plaza of government office buildings proposed by then New York State governor Nelson A. Rockefeller. This plaza was at the time the basis for the largest urban renewal project in the United States. All of this meant that tons and tons of cement—requiring tons and tons of sand—would be needed. That's where Hoogebergh enters the picture.

Earlier in this book, I mentioned that the channel of the Hudson River had been dredged and redredged over the years. In the early 1900s, the river channel was deepened from 12 feet to 30 feet, and in later years, it was further deepened to 40 feet to accommodate huge commercial ocean vessels. Much of the sand from the dredging was deposited on Campbell Island. As a matter of fact, there was so much sand that it formed a 20-foot-high plateau that virtually covered Pixtaway and Campbell Islands and filled in the inlet between them. These are the two islands immediately south of Papscanee Island on which Hoogebergh is located.

With so much of this sand available relatively close to Albany, it was only natural that the owners of Hoogebergh, which had the only access to the sand-rich islands to the south, would be approached for a right of way for sand trucks. A cement company from Rensselaer approached the Staats family for a five-year easement. While several owners were reluctant to agree to this intrusion, the easement was granted, with certain written restrictions to be met. When all was said and done, the overriding issue was income, and money was always in short supply for the family. The conditions were:

- The sand-carrying trucks would not operate on weekends.
- The trucks would never exceed a 15 mph speed limit.
- The cement company would put up a sturdy gate near the entrance to the newly created road leading through the Hoogebergh property to the sand deposits. The gate would be locked at the end of each day.
- Rent for the use of the easement would be paid to the Staats family monthly.

For five years, the sand trucks thundered through the property, often bumper to bumper, creating clouds of dust and endangering family members and visitors with their speed and lack of consideration.

Every one of the four conditions was violated. The truck traffic often ran throughout the entire week. The drivers paid little attention to the speed limit. The gate was seldom closed, let alone locked. And when brother Barent stopped by to collect the monthly rent, he was invariably asked to come back at a later time.

By the end of the easement term, most of the family vowed not to renew it. In the early spring of 1978, the cement company received the word that the easement would not be extended.

The cement company resorted to drastic measures by dumping several truckloads of sand at the entrance to the only access road leading into Hoogeberg. There was no way the family could enter or exit the property. If there had been a fire or a medical emergency, it might have been tragic. The family notified the sheriff, and an injunction was issued, ordering the cement company to remove the wall of sand blocking the road.

The company removed the sand but instituted a lawsuit against the Staats family, claiming that it had a permanent right of way. The case went to court, which amounted to a number of hearings over several weeks.

The Staats family had the good fortune of hiring a young attorney, Richard Piedmont, who was most thorough and creative. His task was to prove that the easement road through the property did not exist prior to the trucking agreement. To prove that the easement road was new, he rented a small airplane and took photos of the new road, and then he compared his photos with ones that were taken from the air back in the 1950s when there was no road. That cinched the case. The judge ruled in favor of the Staatses.

The family learned a valuable lesson from this court case. Since then, the family has steadfastly denied any easement rights requested.

Changes in Ownership — 1982

A search of deeds, bequests, etc., by Rensselaer County lawyer Charles E. Craymer traces Hoogebergh ownership from 1866 through to 1947, listing the owners of that period as:

Philip S. Staats (died 1883) to
Philip S. Staats, Jr. (died 1937) to
Jennie Elliot Staats
William S. Staats (died 1910) to
Elizabeth Staats Schell
Lawrence Anthony Staats (died 1921) to
Lawrence Arthur Staats (died 1932) to
Esther F. Staats
Mabel S. Staats
Mabel Staats Higgins

There had not been any change in ownership status since 1947, when brothers Joachim and Lawrence returned from World War II and bought Hoogebergh from family members.

In 1980, brother Joachim, who had been renting out the north wing of the house, decided that he was no longer interested in owning his one-half share of Hoogebergh. There ensued several months of negotiations with the other owners, and in 1982, Joachim and his wife, Katherine, deeded over their share of the estate to Lawrence and his wife, Torill; Hans Dirzuweit (sister Jane's widower); Barent and his wife, Connie; Bleecker and his wife, Doris; and William and his wife, Sandra.

The negotiations involved a significant sum asked by brother Joachim. At about the same time, the neighboring farmer, James Webb, asked to buy the 40 acres of farm land on the east side of the railroad. In later years, the farmer's health failed, and the Staatses agreed to cancel the mortgage obligation. However, Mr. Webb's 1982 offer provided the funding necessary to buy out brother Joachim.

In 1982, the ownership continued to be a family partnership with all of the legal frailties that are peculiar to partnerships. Two of these are "unlimited liability" and "limited life." The "unlimited liability" aspect became a major concern for the remaining owners. For instance, if one member whose name was on the deed contracted a huge debt (e.g., having to pay off an expensive accident claim or medical bill), all of the property owned by the partners (i.e., Hoogebergh) could be sold to settle the claim.

The "limited life" aspect meant that whenever there was any change of ownership, a new deed would have to be drawn up.

There were other issues of concern. What if another partner asked an astronomical price for his or her share? The family had just barely survived the negotiations with brother Kim and were worried about repeating anything similar in the future.

There had to be a way of circumventing the disadvantages of the existing ownership arrangement. It was at this point that an attorney was consulted.

Hoogebergh Incorporation — 1992

Once more the Staats family were blessed. Our attorney was far-sighted and fair. He had recently negotiated a closed family corporation agreement on a Lake George property and had a number of insights to bring to the family's attention. Much of his expertise was heeded and embodied in the articles of incorporation for Hoogebergh.

Some interesting provisions:

- There would be a total of 200 shares distributed evenly among Hans Dirzuweit, Lawrence and Torill, Barent and Connie, Bleecker and Doris, and William and Sandra. Two hundred was the number chosen because it would not involve too many shares and because it would provide 40 shares to each of the five families.

- Shareholders can transfer their shares only to the direct blood line of Lawrence Arthur Staats and Esther Staats (the eighth generation).

- A shareholder wishing to relinquish ownership could offer shares only to existing shareholders and not to anyone outside of the Staats family.

- A shareholder desiring to sell could ask a *maximum* of $10 for each share owned.

- The five families would divide recurring expenses (taxes and insurance) equally.

- Other expenses involved with Hoogebergh (repairs, etc.) would be paid for as decided by the shareholders at the annual meeting. For the most part, a special assessment is asked from those who directly benefit from an improvement. For instance, the copper roof for the west wing benefited all, and all were assessed equally. A used snowplow truck, however, was paid for by just a few shareholders. In many instances, one or two shareholders have picked up the tab for an acquisition, even though it benefited all shareholders.

- The offices would be President, Vice President, Treasurer, and Secretary.

More than 15 years have passed since the corporation was formed. There have been no legal tests of the validity of the organization. The only instance of a legal nature occurred in 1993 when the property had to be assessed for estate tax purposes upon the death of brother Bleecker. No problems were encountered.

Over the years, a number of issues have arisen resulting in amendments to the by-laws. These were mainly due to oversights at the time of incorporation. Two come to mind:

- What constitutes a majority vote on an issue? It was decided that 80% of shares held would be required to approve.

- What happens if a shareholder cannot pay his or her assessment? The vote was to let the assessment ride for three years, whereupon the shares would have to be transferred within the corporation.

At the end of 2008, there were 22 shareholders, most of whom live within 50 miles of Hoogebergh. There is, however, a shareholder in Philadelphia, one in Kansas, and one in California.

A Visit by the Dutch Ambassador — 1995

In the early 1990s, Hoogeberg was visited by a relative, Dr. James Staats, M.D., a prominent surgeon from Birmingham, Alabama, who was most interested in Staats family history. Jim was a well-traveled doctor who had made friends in many parts of the world. One was the ambassador from the Netherlands. In September of 1995, Jim phoned to say the Dutch ambassador, Adriann Jacobovitch, was coming to the Albany area, and Jim wondered if we might contact Mr. Jacobovitch to show him through Hoogebergh.

What a fine evening we had. The family invited the church minister and the church historian. Our Norwegian sister-in-law suggested that we serve some iced genever (Dutch gin) for the occasion. The gathering over dinner was most enjoyable, followed by conversation around the living room fireplace. Mr. Jacobovitch had previously served as the Netherlands ambassador to the Soviet Union during the days of Nikita Khrushchev and also to South Africa during the years of apartheid. He was most interesting and congenial.

The gathering was so successful that the ambassador made time in his busy schedule to visit First Church in Albany with its historic documents and artifacts dating back to 1642. In the afternoon, he revisited Hoogebergh to meet other Staats family members.

A Dutch TV Film Crew Arrives Unexpectedly — 2009

One April afternoon in 2009, my daughter Jennifer, sister-in-law Torill, and I were toiling away at separate projects on a mid-week afternoon. I was painting window frames, so my attire was speckled. Into the Hoogebergh yard drove two vehicles and out stepped five well-dressed young men. They were a film crew from Holland who were spending a month in eastern New York to film a four-part TV documentary depicting the historic relationship between the state and the Netherlands. The head of the crew was Roel van Dalen, a noteworthy media personality in the Netherlands, according to our Google results. His young assistants were polite and capable, speaking perfect English.

The crew had spent the morning in Albany interviewing Dr. Charles Gehring and others at the New York State Library who were involved in the venerable New Netherland project. They were on their way to Kingston and had decided to travel south on route 9J out of Rensselaer, seeking a road that would lead them to a location where they could get film footage of the Hudson River. Inadvertently, they took a right turn on Staats Island Road and arrived at Hoogebergh.

They were soon told that they had unknowingly taken a road that led to one of the oldest Dutch houses in America. They were delighted!—so much so that they spent two hours filming the house and grounds. They were particularly interested in the older tombstones in the cemetery and asked me to be interviewed as the cameras rolled. To me, it was unnerving because of the thought of making erroneous statements, plus the fact that I looked like a bag of rags.

In late September of 2009, word came from a contact in Holland that the video series had been aired and that the Hoogebergh homestead and cemetery were featured.

CHAPTER VII
SHENANIGANS, ANNUAL OUTINGS, AND CELEBRATIONS

It would be interesting to go back in time and learn about the humor and vitality of past generations. So much of this is not documented. Since the '30s, however, recollections of fun times are still firm.

Arthur's Antics — The clearest example of family humor from the eighth generation is a series of photos of my dad, Arthur Staats, that must have been taken in a photo booth at about the time in his mid-30s when he married Esther.

Strip photos of Lawrence "Arthur" Staats making faces at the camera, circa 1920.

The Hanging — In the late 1930s, the diving platform at the riverfront had two tall pilings, towering some 15 feet above the water level on the north and on the south ends. For support, 20-foot 2 x 6s connected them. One evening, brother Kim strung up a life-like dummy, which hung from the middle of the 2 x 6. From a distance, one would swear there had been a suicide. The dummy was so realistic that in the dawning hours of the following morning, a tugboat came down the river, and the engineer friend of Kim's saw the ghastly image in the morning fog. Some time later, he told Kim that he had docked the tug at Castle-ton and phoned the police to report the suicide!!

Another Hanging — A recollection from before World War II was when brother Larry and his friends got together for some photography fun. With a firm rope, they strung their friend Carl Hartnagel up to a limb of the walnut tree for a faux hanging. Larry stood by clad in a bandit's handkerchief and holding a rifle. Just as the photo was being taken, strangers who had taken the wrong road drove into the yard and witnessed the "hanging." The car screeched to a halt and the wheels spun as the visitors hastily departed.

The horse thief (Carl Hartnagel) left, and the lawman (brother Larry) right, circa 1940.

The Bulldozer Antic — Not to be outdone by older siblings, I saw a unique opportunity for a photo op in the 1980s. A construction company had been doing work on the natural gas pipeline that crosses the Hudson about a mile below Hoogebergh. Since the work took several days, the heavy equipment was left at the pipeline site. Friend David Allen started the machine with no problem, and the result was the somewhat disconcerting photo below.

That's no way to treat a senior citizen! (David Allen and the author, William Staats)

The victim (Dick LeSage), brother-in-law Hans Dirzuweit (center), and the firing squad.

The Firing Squad — Larry and friends and a few members of the family staged a photo of a firing squad. Friend Dick LeSage was blindfolded, and several participants held rifles to their shoulders, simulating execution by firing squad. In a follow-up photo, Dick is resting in peace with his head at the foot of a gravestone as the squad kneels over the "corpse."

Mourners

A moonshiner (Carl Hartnagel) gets his just reward.

The Stabbing: Not to be outdone with hanging and shooting, a touch of stabbing seemed fitting at the time.

Diving from the Day Liner — As a youth, brother Kim had a daring streak. There was an annual Rensselaer Day picnic before World War II, when scores of Rensselaer High School students boarded the paddle-wheeled Day Liner at Albany for a picnic at the city of Kingston some 60 miles south of Albany. On the spur of the moment, brother Kim decided to dive overboard as the Day Liner *Alexander Hamilton* was passing Staats Landing. In the men's room, he asked a friend to take care of his clothes, whereupon he stripped down to his briefs, dashed out of the door, ran along the deck, stood on the railing, and made a successful dive into the Hudson. He then swam to Hoogebergh. Because this was against Day Line and police regulations, brother Kim became a hero to his classmates.

Head Removing: Long before the Texas Chain Saw atrocities, the action had to be done by hand.

Mother warned me never to lose my head.

Jumping Off the Dunn Memorial Bridge — When it came to creating a sensation, brother Bleecker was no slouch. He jumped off the Dunn Memorial Bridge some 40 feet into the Hudson. A buddy waiting in a rowboat retrieved him.

Barge Hopping — Back in the late 1930s and throughout the 1940s, a pleasant summer diversion for the ever-swimming Staats family was barge hopping. At that time, there was a company that shipped tremendous amounts of sand piled on barges, so much so that the gunnels of the barge were only a few inches from the surface of the Hudson. To make matters more enticing, the sand looked to be a fun place to frolic, and the barges moved extremely slowly. Usually a tug would be pulling two or three barges at a time. As the barges approached Hoogebergh, several of us would swim out and climb on board. Then we would enjoy ourselves playing in the sand for about half an hour. By this time, the barge had proceeded upriver a half mile or so, and we would dive off the barge, swim ashore, and walk home. It made a hot, sultry afternoon more interesting.

At times, the tug would have so much slack rope between it and the barge that we would grab onto the rope instead of the barge. That was much more challenging because of the current swirling around the ropes. Naturally, the tugboat employees were afraid we would lose our grip and somehow get caught under the barge, but we had the self confidence not to worry about that. They however, would pitch disposable materials, such as fruit and vegetables, at us in an attempt to dislodge us from our grip on the ropes. Fortunately there was never an accident. Eventually, the slow-moving sand barge traffic drew to a close, leaving us to pursue other excitement.

Viking Funerals — After brother Larry brought home his bride, Torill, from Norway in 1977, the family became more familiar with Nordic traditions. In the days of the Vikings, when a man died, his body was placed in his favorite boat, which was then set afire and pushed out into the fjord, where the remains were cremated. At Hoogebergh, we simulated this Viking funeral tradition at several parties. Our version was to make a dummy of straw, place it in a well-worn wooden boat, and soak it with kerosene. As evening approached, the boat would be set afire and pushed out into the Hudson. It certainly was a novel experience for party goers.

After several of these awesome funerals, it all came to an end when the boat, blazing merrily, floated far out into the channel of the Hudson River just as a huge oil tanker approached Staats Island. There was a flurry of activity as several swimmers successfully sank the boat before the ship got too close.

Diving from the Buoy: The Coast Guard buoy in the river near Hoogebergh has always been a temptation, even though the Coast Guard frowns upon anyone encroaching on its property. Hence "forbidden fruit" presents an irresistible allure to the Staats family and friends. Climbing it, prying friends loose from it and pushing them into the water, diving from the top, etc., are fun. The combined weight of two or three participants can bring the buoy almost to a horizontal position.

Son Grant dives from a buoy.

A Tradition of Terrific Parties

Over the decades, Hoogebergh has been the site for literally dozens of festive occasions, including holiday picnics, song fests, weddings and receptions, bachelor parties, and usually a special annual event where dozens of family and friends join forces to celebrate.

Christmas Parties — Since 1956, there has been an annual Christmas party. Attendees bring along snacks and beverages, and the family provides sandwiches and coffee. As many as 80 multi-generationals will join in the fun, which includes conversation, socializing, and singing Christmas carols and other old-time favorites around the piano. Now and then, a young guest will perform on a musical instrument. The pool table is covered with plywood on which the food is placed. Once the crowd diminishes in the late hours, the plywood is removed and billiard competition begins. Those not playing or observing in the pool room will usually gather around the living room fireplace for conversation—sometimes until the daylight hours.

Halloween Parties — From the mid-1950s through the late 1970s, there was an annual Halloween party at the homestead. Most of them involved costumes. There were always food and refreshments and games involving all attendees. Some 20 guests participated in the fun-making into the late hours of the evening. Old chestnuts such as scavenger hunts and pin-the-tail-on-thedonkey were often revived along with the introduction of new activities each year. Often attendees sang limericks and put on performances. Wil Koveleskie's "Toast to Cardinal Puff" and Fred Hutchinson's "Blowing Out the Candle" routines were particularly popular.

In subsequent years, there have been intermittent Halloween parties as the tenth generation matured and exhibited creativity. In 2008, I appeared dressed provocatively as an aging "Chippendale"—some sight for a 76-year-old!

Holiday Get-togethers — Summer holidays—Memorial Day, July 4, and Labor Day—are popular times for gathering together family and friends. The spacious grounds and availability of sports and other recreational facilities provide an ideal setting, often enjoyed each day of the long weekends. Attendees pool offerings of food and refreshments.

Bachelor Parties — There have been several of these over the past several decades. I will avoid giving details, but I can say that they often last until daylight hours and usually involve sports (softball, croquet) and sometimes swimming. Fortunately, there has never been an accident or an arrest or women involved.

Three of these parties come to mind. One summer afternoon, a softball game ensued. Two of the teammates were such strong batters that brother Barry was swimming several feet off shore with a catcher's mitt in his hand. At another party, a son-in-law-to-be was left fully clothed and clinging to a buoy far out in the Hudson well after midnight. The party for brother Larry (soon to marry a Norwegian) found participants sipping vodka and aquavit until daylight—so much so that many simply fell asleep on the front lawn, lying prostrate where they dropped off. The following morning, the several inert bodies strewn about somewhat resembled a Civil War battlefield scene.

The Annual Work Weekend — The last weekend in April is set aside for combining the efforts of family and friends to spruce up Hoogebergh for the forthcoming warm weather months. A list, sometimes as long as five pages, is developed in advance of the weekend. Routine tasks such as raking, painting, closet cleaning, and dish washing are on the list, as well as special projects that are often tackled by small groups of attendees. Some years ago, several people helped plant 2,000 evergreen trees. Outdoor sheds have been constructed, cement floors poured, and outdoor fireplaces rebuilt on these weekends. It is amazing what can be accomplished when several people pool their efforts.

This is also the time for great conversation and sumptuous barbeques. Since Hoogebergh was incorporated, work weekend has also been the time of the annual meeting of the shareholders.

The Summer "Special Blasts" — Each summer, one or two special occasions demand the efforts of several to organize and carry out the event. These include graduation parties, weddings, receptions, anniversaries, and special birthday celebrations. In recent years, there has been an annual summer "bash" with a theme. Often as many as a dozen souls are involved in the preparation, and attendance can number anywhere between 50 and 250. These summer celebrations started in the 1960s and have continued to the present.

In the '60s, '70s and '80s, when the ninth generation was mostly involved, the parties would seldom have attendance in excess of 80. When the tenth generation took over in the late '90s, parties with more than 100 attending have been the rule. There have been several pig roasts, luaus, steak roasts, and on one occasion, the roast of a beef quarter. Once in a while, the food service is catered, but for the most part, family and friends have been directly involved.

Party-goers await instructions for the next event on the day's agenda.

Most of the summer special gatherings have featured live music, but now and then a DJ has been used. These parties involve an assessment for all attendees, since the cost to the host would be prohibitive. Even so, an assessment of $20 or $25 for an event that includes food, beverages, musical entertainment, games, etc., is not a bad bargain for participants. People are encouraged to bed down in tents rather than attempt the hazards of driving home afterwards.

One advantage of having a large group sleep over in tents is the availability of help to clean up after the party the following morning. The tradition is to have Hoogebergh appear as though there had never been a party by noon on the following day. With the help of many hands tidying, carting trash, putting away tarps, etc., the cleanup seems to get done effortlessly.

Some of the more memorable of these occasions have been:

- **1988—Champagne Celebration** Guests attended in semi-formal attire. Champagne tables were set up at several locations. Tiki torches glowed as evening set in. Dancing took place on the deck. The tour boat *Dutch Apple* paused to allow passengers time to view the activities.

- **1991—Luau** Guests appeared in colorful attire, including grass skirts and sarongs. Hawaiian friend Sophie Leary gave hula demonstrations and lessons to an enthusiastic group on the dance floor. A croquet game under the lights was an after-midnight treat.

- **1992—Karaoke Party** After a catered feast of wings, corn, meatballs, and salad, several participants took turns at the microphone, assisted by a DJ. Some were awful, some not so bad, and some exceeded all expectations.

- **1993—Pirate Party** Some 70 guests attended in costume. The main entertainment was a 1Y2-hour search for a key following a series of clues. The key unlocked a box containing prizes. As expected, there was considerable mischief—including downright cheating—but it was all in fun.

- **1996—Mad Cow Disease Party** This featured the roasting of a steamboat round on a spit. During the party, a two-hour power outage canceled all lighting except tiki torches and candles. Fortunately, the electrically powered spit had already done its job, and there was ample time for conversation and games after the feast and before the dancing started.

Sophie Leary gives hula lessons at the 1991 Luau.

- **1998—Surprise 75th Birthday Party for Brother Larry** This party was such a successful surprise that brother Larry kept asking why so many out-of-town friends had arrived. It was well into the evening before someone told him the purpose of the party. Testimonial speeches, a slide show, and a DJ rounded out an entertaining evening. In fact, two couples, unknown to any of us, made a wrong turn and arrived at the party in error. They were so enamored by the festivities that they asked permission to remain.
- **2001—Survivor Party** Some 160 guests attended a thoroughly organized party starting off with a pig roast. Games included a scavenger hunt, relay races, balloon races, tug of war, and Trivial Pursuit.
- **2002—Nautical Theme Party** Steamed clams, fresh corn, salads, and chicken were provided for consumption. Games included basketball on the raft, a relay race with glasses of water, a treasure hunt, and tug of war. A DJ supplied the music. It was such a warm evening that several took the opportunity to swim in the Hudson just to cool off.
- **2004—Wild West Party** Artistic niece Ingrid created a huge faux saguaro cactus. Creative costumes abounded, including me dressed in a filthy T-shirt with strips of bacon pinned to it: the disguise of the chuck wagon cook. Contests included bow and arrow shooting at targets, spitting water-melon seeds for distance records, and

construction of bows and arrows from bare essentials of sticks and string.

- **2005—Caribbean Theme Party** Some 150 guests enjoyed tropical food and a contest involving passing bananas from person to person in lines without using the hands.

- **2006—'50s Theme Party and Surprise 80th Birthday Party for Brother Barry** Some 150 guests attended wearing very creative costumes, including a few versions of Elvis. Daughter Giss built a huge birthday cake mounted on a cart, which was towed onto the party scene in the late hours. An attractive female guest, after thinking over bouncing out of the cake, declined the opportunity, so I, dressed in a frumpy red dress, red wig, and old lady's hat, did the honors. It was so startling and ugly that brother Barry thought there must have been some awful mistake.

- **2009—Gazebo Celebration Party** Brother Barry had an idea to have a large gazebo built on the terrace overlooking the river. It has been a smashing success, providing a fine view of the Hudson with shelter from light rain and burning sun. To celebrate completion of the structure, about 220 people attended a most successful evening of feasting, entertainment, and partying until dawn.

The author as King Neptune at the "Nautical Theme Party"

Music was provided by the most successful band in the Capital District area, "The Refrigerators." with whom 83-year-old brother Barry has become a "groupie." The guys provided amazing entertainment and excellent music for dancing. For hours there were at least 80 people dancing on the deck. It's a wonder the structure survived!

With such a large group of guests, we anticipated some disturbances, but all went amazingly well. Volunteer attendees cooked chicken and corn, and a buffet line moved along smoothly. In the midnight hours, when hunger set in once again, a feast of chicken wings was put on the table.

Control at the entrance gate was phenomenal. A computerized, alphabetized list of attendees who had paid or promised to pay upon arrival was strictly adhered to by family and friends.

About 20 tents were set up, and the weather was perfect. That was an unexpected treat, since June and July were the rainiest months in years. While there were no contests and games, the casual conversation and dancing passed the time quickly. The effort involved in the preparations, however, took weeks.

"The Refrigerators" perform at the Gazebo celebration.

CHAPTER VIII
REMEMBRANCES FROM THE NINTH GENERATION

Ghosts

Categorically, there are no ghosts at Hoogeberg. **PERIOD.**

However, rumors of ghosts persist each time something new and strange is sensed. I'm sure the ghost stories go back much further than 1948, which is when Louis C. Jones published *Spooks of the Valley* (Houghton Mifflin Company-Boston) a story for early teenagers centered at Hoogebergh. Although 60 years have passed, the local junior high school will occasionally schedule tours, and some curious youngster will ask about George, the ghost who was buried under the wood pile.

There have been sightings, to be sure. Niece Cheryl stands firm on her conviction that "Grandma Breese," wearing a family brooch, appeared before her in the living room.

The cover for Louis C. Jones' book

— ACKNOWLEDGMENTS —

I want to thank Mrs. Esther Staats for permission to use and haunt the old Staats House. Now that peace has come, her sons are living in the house again. "It means," their mother wrote me recently, "that the Staats house will carry on." This is as it should be, for there are not many families in America who have lived three hundred years in the house their ancestors built. Long may they live on the land and in the house they love — unhaunted.

Author Louis C. Jones thanks Esther Staats for permission to haunt Hoogebergh.

Son-in-law Craig asserts that on the edge of the parking lot, he saw a vision of a man wearing a Civil War uniform. Even I, who swears there are no ghosts, saw in the northwest bedroom at midnight what appeared to be a spiraling cloud of material shaped like a human being.

Sister Jane used to tell of the Sunday 'evening after the veterans had returned from World War II, when a small group was gathered around the living room at night at Hoogebergh, listening to the radio in total darkness. There came a distinctive "thud" behind the downstairs door leading into the west wing—and every person in the room arose and silently abandoned the house, driving away in terror.

Sketch of Hoogeberg used in the book

The Night I Was a Ghost

One of my favorite recollections is the night I unexpectedly had the opportunity to be a ghost. It was around 2 a.m. on a balmy summer night, and I was reading in the upstairs master bedroom because I had awakened and could not get back to sleep. Suddenly a car drove into the parking lot, and I instantly recognized my nephew Chip's voice and also that of a girl he must have brought along on a date. Not wanting to interfere with Chip's plans, I turned off the bedroom lamp.

"What was that?" the girl asked. "I just saw a light go off in that second story room!" Chip assured her that she had imagined it, but he could not persuade her to go into the house. It was a clear moonlight night, and my car was hidden away at the lower parking lot, so it looked as though Hoogebergh had no one in residence.

Once I realized that the girl was frightened out of her wits, I decided to go a step further. I quietly stole from the master bedroom into the southwest bedroom in the west wing. By this time, Chip had persuaded his lady friend to stroll down to the diving platform to have a look at the river. I could hear them chatting amiably in the moonlight. That's when I turned the bedroom light on.

Instantly the girl reacted. "A light just went on in that upstairs bedroom. It was dark when we came down here. I want to go home —right now!"

The tall bedroom windows (12 panes in each) in which a "ghost" or a "mummy" might make an unexpected appearance.

Chip had no choice but to take the girl back to the car, but first they had to walk up the hill past the front of the house. Stealthily, I sneaked back to the master bedroom, wrapped myself in a sleeping bag, and stood up in the full-length window. Then I reached behind me and switched the light back on. To all appearances I looked like a mummy standing in the window.

There was a scream and a scurrying of feet and then the sound of the car door slamming shut. The ruse had definitely worked!

Chip mustered up the courage to get out of the car and walk back to the front of the house. Looking at the upstairs bedroom, he bravely shouted, "I don't know who you are up there but I want you know that I resent the fact that you scared the (expletive) out of my date!" With that, he stormed back to the car and the twosome hastily drove away.

For years, Chip blamed a young family friend—until eventually I confessed.

Hauntings

It hasn't helped that over the years, several deliberate "haunting" incidents have been staged for young teenagers having Hoogebergh sleepovers. The haunting has been done by older brothers and their friends. For instance, when tenth-generation Heather and several girlfriends in their early teens were staying overnight, older brother Grant and his buddy stealthily climbed onto the house roof and lowered long chains down the chimney into the fireplace in the living room where the girls were bedding down for the night. When the chains rattled, the girls were terrified. When they bolted for the door, a hideous masked face appeared in the window. Moans and screams added to the terror. Needless to say, the parents were not pleased.

It also hasn't helped that over the years when the tenth generation were very young, outdoor nighttime fireplace stories would often turn into ghost story sessions. "The Monkey's Paw," "The Bandingly Hotel," and "I Want My Toe"—always told using Hoogebergh as the setting—were favorites. They must have worked, because to this day, few of the tenth generation, now in their 40s, will stay overnight alone at Hoogebergh.

Memorable Incidents

The Pancake Incident: In our earlier years, when Mother was not able to be at Hoogebergh, she would delegate an older sibling to take care of the younger ones. Some took on the assignment with a vengeance. So it was that at the ripe old age of 15, brother Kim (Joachim) was directed to take charge of brother Bleecker (age 10) and me (age 7).

For breakfast, Kim cooked a batch of pancakes for us. It became a gigantic stack, and we were really famished. That's when we discovered that there wasn't any syrup or butter in the house. Hoogebergh was far removed from food sources, so Kim exercised his coveted authority and ordered his younger brothers to eat all of the dry, slightly burned pancakes. At first we refused, but the older brother was a force to be reckoned with. So we gagged down a pancake or two.

Satisfied that we were obeying orders, Kim stepped out of the kitchen to go to the barn and bring back an armload of firewood for the kitchen stove. No sooner was he out the door than brother Bleecker seized the opportunity. He took the lid off the wood stove and dumped his stack of dry pancakes onto the hot coals. Unfortunately, Kim returned sooner than expected with the armload of wood. When he took the lid off the stove, behold: there was Bleek's smoldering stack of pancakes.

That's when brother Bleek and I learned the wrath of an older brother.

Larry and the Skunk: A few years ago, brother Larry was becoming more and more annoyed with a critter that was creeping into the garage at night and feasting on the contents of the cat's feeding dish. He eventually decided to take action, and he set a "have a heart" trap to catch the intruder.

It worked. The next morning there was a skunk in the trap. He had to be handled cautiously, but Larry put the trap (suspended on a long pole) into his truck and transported the skunk to a destination about two miles south of Hoogebergh. Just to be sure he was rid of invaders, however, Larry once again set the trap.

The next morning there was another skunk. Larry followed the same routine that he had with the first one, releasing the animal at a remote location. Lo and behold, the next morning there was yet a third skunk, and away it was carted.

On the fourth morning, yet another skunk cringed in the trap. This time around, Larry became suspicious. He squirted some red spray paint into the cage on the white strip on the skunk's back and then took it for a ride.

On the fifth morning, the trap once more held a skunk. This one, however, had red paint on its white stripe. This time around, Larry drove the repeat offender far, far away.

Larry and the Llama: For a few years, brother Barry owned a llama that he had purchased from a local game farm as a pet for his daughter. The beast had an ugly disposition, which seemed to get uglier as it grew older and bigger. At maturity, it weighed several hundred pounds and was not to be trusted. Sturdy fencing was necessary. When Barry and his family took their annual week of vacation at Cape Cod in early September, he asked Larry to look after the llama. This only required feeding it pellets and providing a daily pail of water.

In the late afternoon, Larry filled a container of pellets and put it in front of the animal. It began munching away, happily. Then it paused, raised its head, and stared at Larry while still munching its pellets. Then it did something Larry never expected (although it is a known habit of llamas, camels, alpacas, and the like). It spit its mouthful of chewed pellets directly into Larry's face.

Not liking the beast in the first place, Larry immediately took revenge. He plunged his head into the llama's waiting bucket of drinking water and filled his cheeks as much as they would hold. When the llama once again raised its head to stare at him, he spewed his mouthful of water directly into its eyes. The llama retreated at a good pace to the far side of its pen.

Larry and the Raccoons: In the mid-1980s, the area around Hoogebergh became infested with rabid raccoons. The animals, which are almost always nocturnal, would appear in broad daylight, unafraid of humans where previously they had been noted for shyness. I recall an incident when I was painting a glider swing I had purchased. It was near a wooded area. A raccoon staggered out of the weeds and began to snarl. At the time, I had no idea about the rabies epidemic, but I did know that this unusual behavior was something to be concerned about. I temporarily abandoned the paint job.

The animals became so bold that they would literally tear though window screens when they scented food in the house. We had to put heavy-duty screens on for protection.

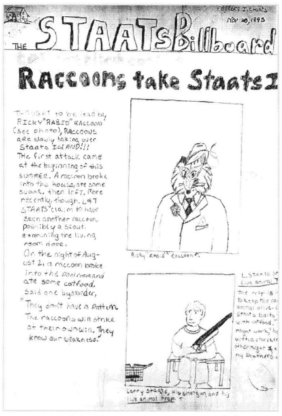

Cartoon of "Ricky" the raccoon and brother Larry drawn by Larry's creative 11-year-old daughter, Ingrid.

Brother Larry was not one to put up with an assault by rabid animals. On one occasion, he patiently sat on the veranda with a .22 caliber rifle in his lap, awaiting the appearance of a raccoon. One appeared, all right. It came around the corner of the veranda and sat watching Larry with the gun in his lap.

There has since been an interesting twist to this incident. Brother Larry, who died in the summer of 2008, was cremated and buried in the cemetery at Hoogebergh, next to the graves of brother Bleecker, brother Kim, and sister-in-law, Sandra. For 10 years, no animal had ever tampered with those gravesites—until Larry was interred.

In the spring of 2009, Larry's wife noticed animal diggings around Larry's gravesite. After trying a number of tactics to discourage the digging, she set a "have-a-heart" meshed trap. On two occasions, she captured a raccoon!

Adrift on an Ice Pan: At about age 10, I was exploring the ice along the river shore with my older brother Bleek and next door neighbor Joe Podoba. It was about the time when the ice was breaking up as spring approached. Several large ice pans were more of a temptation than we boys could resist. We went to the boat storage area where we sneaked out two oars and then headed back to the river shore. At the time we were dressed for winter: hats, gloves, snowsuits, and boots. Bleek, Joe, and I fearlessly stepped onto a nearby ice cake and, using the oars, steered it slowly away from shore and out toward the channel. It seemed so exciting. Suddenly, the ice pan broke into two pieces, leaving Bleek and Joe and the two oars on one cake. They were able to steer their ice pan close enough to shore to step off safely.

Two grownups floating on an ice pan in the Hudson.

Not me. My cake of ice drifted with the current farther and farther out into the river, steadily moving south and away from shore. Bleek and Joe followed along the shore, voicing support but unable to help me. I was approaching a state of panic. When my ice pan passed the diving platform, I seized the moment and jumped into the river to swim to shore, in spite of soaking my hat, gloves, snowsuit, and boots. Ah, was that water cold!

And brother Bleek's comment when I dragged myself out of the water? "Boy, did you look funny flopping around like that with all of your clothes on." I was too relieved to stay angry.

A Tree Falls on the Outhouse: In the early 1990s, before the compost toilet was built, there was only one outhouse near Hoogebergh. One afternoon, a number of us were together on the veranda, watching a gathering storm. Good friends had come for a visit. "Before the storm hits, I think I should pay a visit," Jean said, using terminology commonly associated with visiting the john. While she was in the outdoor toilet, the storm hit in full force with winds gusting to 92 mph. Suddenly the century-old black walnut tree, which had provided shade for the house for decades, broke at the base from the force of the wind, and came crashing down, right on the outhouse. Jean was trapped inside.

Her husband and I fought our way through the fallen limbs and foliage, using the chain saw on the larger barriers to the outhouse. The door opened and out stepped Jean, shaken but unscathed. After rehashing the incident several times, Jim and Jean departed.

The next day, a mutual friend phoned to ask the condition of the outhouse. "How did you know about that?" I inquired. "Well," she responded, "I was at our church meeting last evening, and Jean Burns offered a prayer of thanksgiving for her safe rescue from an outdoor toilet that had been landed on by a fallen tree." That story will live on forever.

Unforgettable Personalities

Esther's Suitor

Through a friend from church, Mother developed a relationship with Frank, an East Greenbush farmer, when she was in her late 40s and most of us siblings were in our teens. Needless to say, the suitor was eyed with suspicion and apprehension by the ninth generation.

As well he should have been. For one thing, he owned a significant acreage of fields used for growing hay. In mid-summer, Frank suggested we all come to his farm for the day. Mother crammed us all into the car and to the farm we went. When we got there, Frank had the hay wagon ready and eagerly awaited the bull work of several unsuspecting teenagers to load the wagon with bales of hay. It was hot and exhausting work. At this point we had a right to be suspicious. We were being thought of as cheap labor.

Frank was cheap. He often used the expression "take care of the dimes and the dollars will take care of themselves." On one occasion, he treated several of us youngsters to a trip to a petting zoo in Albany. There were woodchucks, beavers, rabbits, squirrels, hamsters, guinea pigs—nothing spectacular. At the end of the exhibits was a box with a sign "please leave something to buy food for the animals." Big-hearted Frank gave us each a penny to put into the box.

In those days, there was no phone at Hoogebergh, so visits were spontaneous. Somehow Frank always managed to show up at dinner time. Brother Bleek swears that in wintertime there was a bare spot in the snow on the road leading to the house—made by Frank's car as he waited for supper to be put on the table.

When Frank said grace, we all bowed our heads and endured an endless prayer. It seemed that by the time he finished, the only food that wasn't cold was the ice cream.

Thoughtful and caring? Once Frank took Mother to a movie that ended after dark. It was early spring, and when they arrived at the end of the road leading into Hoogebergh, they discovered that the road was covered with two or more feet of flood water. Frank opened the trunk of his car, took out pair of hip boots, and handed them to Mother. He then drove away, leaving her to manage the perilous trek across the flooded road. The next time he came to visit, he greeted Mother, "Esther, it's so good to see you looking well. When I last saw you, you were wading across the road in the dark. I thought I heard you cry out, but I assumed that you had the strength to manage the crossing."

After a few years of putting up with Frank and also the disparaging comments of her offspring, Mother finally drew the relationship to a screeching halt. The last straw was an automobile accident. Frank had bought a brand new brown Nash, which was one of the first cars with hydraulic brakes. Mother was driving and Frank was in the passenger seat. Two older friends, the Caulkins (in their 80s) were riding in the back seat. As she was descending a steep hill in upper Rensselaer, the hydraulic brakes failed, and the car sped downhill and crashed into a sturdy tree at the bottom of the hill. Mother suffered a broken finger. Both of the Caulkins were killed. Frank was shaken but uninjured. When he surveyed the damage, he exclaimed, "Good Lord, look what has happened to my new car!"

That was the last time she had anything to do with Frank. Regarding the Caulkins, her comment was consistent with her practical nature. After she adjusted to the loss of these dear friends, she said, "Well, you know, they always wanted to go together. The Lord answered their wish."

Esther's Closest Friend

She wasn't related to us in any way, but we always called her Aunt Tell. Her name was Bertelle, and she was Mom's closest friend for many years. If fact, when Mother and Arthur decided to marry, she phoned Aunt Tell and asked, "Are you busy this afternoon? Arthur and I have decided to get married, and I want to you be maid of honor...at 4 p.m. if you can make it."

By profession, Aunt Tell was a librarian in the Van Rensselaer High School. She was a maiden lady and started out by teaching English for the grand sum of $900 a year. Incredibly, the administration asked her to take a cut in pay the second year because they were low on funds. She stayed on the job for several decades. She loved books, and each Christmas, she gave my siblings and me an autographed book that she knew we should read.

We loved her. Her interests were broad, and she traveled during the summer months, often with close teaching friends. In the mid-1930s, five of them toured the United States, stopping at Yellowstone National Park and other interesting sights. In those days, accommodations consisted of separate tourist cabins owned by private entrepreneurs. At one point, they stopped at a gas station near Death Valley, and the elderly attendant poked his head through the side window and looked the ladies over. Then he commented, "I just wanted to see five ladies who have been traveling together for some time and are still speaking to each other."

After she retired, she would spend months traveling as a passenger on cargo ships. In those days, for extra money, the shipping companies had berths on board for half a dozen passengers. It was an intimate way to travel, and the food was good. However, the passengers were at the mercy of the ship's schedule. It wouldn't be unusual for the ship to change course after receiving notice that they should proceed to a different destination than planned. As a result, Aunt Tell's traveling stories were thrilling.

When my wife and I traveled to Melbourne, Australia, to take a one-year college teaching assignment in 1965, we were contacted by Aunt Tell, then in her late 60s. She wondered if she could visit us in Australia, and we were delighted, in spite of the fact that we were ensconced in a small house with our four children. For two nights, she stayed at a hotel in downtown Melbourne, until we begged her to come and stay with us in the suburbs, reasoning that our accommodations were free and that it would allow us to spend more time together. Not wishing to impose, she reluctantly agreed, with the proviso that we would first pay a visit to a liquor store. She bought a gallon of sherry, and we enjoyed several days of her company, merrily sipping wine on the front porch before supper was ready.

Then she was off to Tasmania and to Adelaide. When she returned, we had her join us for an afternoon at the beach house of the Hulls, my Australian department chairman and his young family. The afternoon was huge success, so much so that Aunt Tell asked to treat the Hulls and my wife to dinner at a prominent hotel in Melbourne.

That, too, was a successful occasion. Brandy flowed before, during, and after dinner. During dinner, Aunt Tell said, "I want to tell you about my recent retirement party" and proceeded on with oh so many complete details, voice inflections, and hand gestures. It was a fun story, and we listened attentively. Not more than five minutes after she completed the retirement story, she said, "I want to tell you about my recent retirement party" and then proceeded to relate the exact story she had previously told, using the same voice inflections and hand gestures. Apparently the brandy had kicked in. We all listened politely, but we were shaking with mirth. Allen Hulls laughed so hard tears were falling into his lap. His wife, Elizabeth, leaned over to me and whispered, "Haven't we heard all of this before?" in her rich Australian accent. It had to be one of the funniest memories of my life.

When the dinner was over, we took the elevator to the ground floor and proceeded to walk to the car. For support, I took Aunt Tell's right arm because she was unsteady on her feet. She said somewhat indignantly, "You don't have to take my arm. I can manage perfectly well by myself." Whereupon I released my grip and she proceeded to veer to her left and walk into a brick wall. What a fun night!

The culmination of that most successful occasion was Aunt Tell's invitation to the Hulls to come to America and stay at her home for free for as long as they pleased. Four years later, the Australian family arrived in Rensselaer as he took on a teaching assignment in my college's accounting department. The wonderful year could not have occurred without the generous offer of housing by Aunt Tell.

Aunt Gail

My mother was from a family of five Scots-Irish WASPs. It was a shock to the family when her brother, Uncle Allen, a veteran of WWI and a bachelor until his mid-40s, married Aunt Gail, a Roman Catholic of Italian descent who happened to be—worst of all—divorced.

Uncle Allen was a favorite with the ninth generation because of his kindly nature and his love for children. He lived at Hoogebergh during summers for several of his bachelor years when he worked as a conductor on the railroad. On the basis of his good-natured manner, Aunt Gail had to be welcomed despite reservations about her background.

Aunt Gail was tall, dark haired, striking in appearance, and well dressed. Every hair was always in place and tinted jet black. She had a great sense of humor, and hypochondria and a severe tendency to stretch the truth were her main drawbacks. She was a fine cook. She had a part-time job in the cosmetics department of a pharmacy. As with so many who grew up in the depression years, Aunt Gail and Uncle Allen never owned a home but always rented an apartment. Her taste in home decorations was flawless.

My earliest recollections of Aunt Gail were the many evenings of pinochle with her, Uncle Allen, and my mother. In the late hours, for a break, Aunt Gail would make coffee, Italian style. It was so thick and black that getting a spoon to sink to the bottom of the cup was almost impossible.

Aunt Gail Smith

Her exaggerations and tall stories pervaded the conversation. Mother would just nod in agreement and wink to the others. "Esther, I was so sick that day that I dropped to my knees and crawled five blocks to the house through the snow!" she once said with a perfectly straight face.

She had little use for her son-in-law, whom she called the "lazy Dutchman." "Esther, he lost his temper and chased me up the stairs," she said. "When I got to the top, I turned around and belted him so hard that he tumbled to the bottom." We were expected to believe all of this.

Eventually Uncle Allen died. Mother predicted that at sometime during the funeral service Aunt Gail would faint. It was a cold February day when Uncle Allen was buried. Because he was a veteran, a flag was draped over his coffin. At the end of the graveside service, as is customary, the funeral director handed the folded flag to Aunt Gail, and right on cue, she raised her hand to her brow and dropped to the ground in a dead faint. Mother's prediction was right on the mark.

As the years passed, Aunt Gail's health deteriorated. I'm sure her mini-heart attacks were serious, but there were ever so many of them over the years, and she seemed to enjoy talking about them. Eventually she passed away in her mid-80s. I asked her grandson at the wake just how many heart attacks she had complained of over the years. "It must have been at least two or three hundred," was his considered response.

Mr. Keyer

In the 1930s, a Dutchman named Claus Keyer, a handyman, stayed next door to Hoogebergh in a shack on the grounds of the Gerritt Staats house. Apparently, as a young man he was a sailor who came to New York from Amsterdam and "jumped ship" to stay in the USA. He had a wife (whom we seldom saw) and a son who lived in Castleton. Apparently he wasn't very close with his family. He liked to drink beer or homemade wine or whatever he could lay his hands on.

After my father died in 1932, Mr. Keyer would often help Mother with a variety of jobs. To me, he was old, short, thin, and bow-legged, and he had a high squeaky voice. He loved young children, and he had a great sense of humor. On Sunday mornings, he would get out the pancake griddle, a huge cast iron circular pan some two feet in diameter with a handle. It was a special treat when he made pancakes. After the family was fed, Mr. Keyer would take the remaining pancake batter and completely fill the griddle, making a huge pancake. "This one is for Kaiser!" he'd announce. Kaiser was his large, brown, friendly, curly-haired collie-police dog mix.

With his drinking problem, he was in one car wreck after another. Fortunately, no one was ever seriously injured. Somewhere along the way, he acquired a 1931 Model A Ford Deluxe Roadster and managed to avoid wrecking it. That's the car he sold to my mother when the police finally told him that he had to choose between drinking and driving.

The Czech farmer who bought the Gerritt Staats house, Mike Podoba, would also use Mr. Keyer as a handyman. After becoming successful, Mike would periodically buy a large, new car at the end of harvest season when he knew whether he could afford to pay for it. He always paid in cash. He trusted the Dutchman to the extent that he would occasionally let the old man drive his car.

On one occasion, Mr. Keyer asked my older brother Larry to ride with him on a trip to Rensselaer. The car was a brand new, expensive Chrysler and had the innovation of a cigarette lighter on the dashboard. Mr. Keyer smoked cigarettes and proceeded to put one in his mouth as he was driving along. Ordinarily those who smoked would strike a match, light the cigarette, and then toss the match out of the window, weather permitting. Mr. Keyer followed the usual routine, except with the dashboard lighter. Once the cigarette was going, he instinctively shook the lighter and tossed it out the window as one would do with a match. It disappeared into the swamp bordering the highway. Despite a desperate search, the lighter was never found. Mike Podoba wasn't pleased.

The old Dutch handyman had a great sense of humor. One time he decided to use "shock and awe" on some guys who were fishing in the Hudson from the diving platform. They had caught a white perch and had put it in a pail of water. Mr. Keyer ambled onto the platform and asked how the fishermen were doing. They proudly pointed to the fish swimming around in the pail of water, whereupon Mr. Keyer reached into the pail, picked up the live fish, and proceeded to take a generous bite out of its belly! Spitting out his mouthful of fish, he remarked, "Ain't too sweet!" and turned and walked off the platform, chuckling to himself. The guys were aghast.

In later years, Mr. Keyer moved to another part of the state to find work. Occasionally, he would stop by Hoogebergh when he was in the area visiting his son. We learned that he lived to the age of 89—a remarkable feat for a man who consumed so much alcohol.

Uncle Will and Aunt Bessie

It must have been traumatic for Uncle Will and Aunt Bessie to take their bereaved sister's six children into their small rented home weekdays throughout the fall, winter, and spring. My siblings and I were lucky not to have been assigned to foster homes. In our family, Uncle Will and Aunt Bessie were regarded as saints to be respected and obeyed.

Uncle Will was a railroad engineer for the New York Central Railroad in the 1920s through the early 1940s, when asthma forced him to retire. His asthma was so severe that he spent most of his later life in a reclining chair for sleeping, since lying prone on a bed made it difficult for him to breathe.

There are so many great memories of that terrific guy. On the Fourth of July, he would always arrive at Hoogebergh with a car full of a variety of fireworks, and they would be set off throughout the day. He gave us an allowance of 25 cents a month, and in those days, it was like receiving gold.

He was capable of occasionally letting out a string of oaths—so well put together that it was almost poetic.

He chewed tobacco, a brand called Havana Blossom-plain. It was rationed during World War II, but we managed to keep him stocked up. He had a spittoon in the poolroom at Hoogebergh and next to his chair in the Rensselaer house. The spittoon was set on opened newspapers because his tobacco-spitting wasn't all that accurate. Before he retired, he drove a big 1920s Oldmobile sedan. The driver's side window and door had tobacco stain trails running down them.

The Air Raid Drill: Air raid drills during World War II were the bane of his existence. When the siren sounded, all lights in the house were to be immediately turned off. If not, a volunteer warden would knock on the door and tell you to shut off the lights. One time, a sudden wail of the siren caught Uncle Will by surprise. He was standing by his reclining chair, but when he shut off the light and began to sit, he missed the chair and sat in the half-filled spittoon. The string of oaths could be heard for several blocks.

When he worked, Uncle Will invariably donned a set of bib overalls, which had at least eight pockets. In these, he would store nails, screws, measuring tape, etc., and also a tobacco pouch. As his work progressed, he would reach into the pockets of his overalls with great deliberation, searching for whatever he needed. First his hand would go into one pocket and then another and then another—until he just happened to feel that tobacco pouch. At that point, he would pull out the pouch, tuck a generous helping into his cheek to make a cud, and then chew with satisfaction. If a helper were at hand, he would wink and then search the other pockets until he found what he was originally looking for.

Uncle William Ledger Smith, age 60, circa 1950.

The $500 Chair: We had an antique rush-bottom chair that Aunt Bessie cherished. It was strictly for show and not for sitting. Once Uncle Will, who was considerably overweight, made the mistake of sitting in the chair, and it collapsed under him, leaving him sitting on the floor.

"Will, is that the $500 antique chair?" Aunt Bessie called out from the next room. To which he replied, "If it is, it's not worth a nickel now!"

Drying Himself in Public View: When he got into his 50s and 60s, Uncle Will had a good-sized belly. On one occasion, he had taken a bath (we never had a shower) and was standing near the bathroom window, which overlooked the street. Even though the shade was pulled, his silhouette was clearly visible from the street. Aunt Bessie just happened to be passing by the house when she looked up and was horrified by the sight of her brother's display. She rushed into the house and called out, "Will, get away from the window. People can clearly see you drying yourself!" He answered, "What's the matter—ain't I got shape?

Phone Rationing: Uncle Will was almost always good natured, but he was also strict. Because he worked on the railroad and would be contacted by phone when he was scheduled to work, the rest of the family was warned to use the only phone in the house very sparingly. To this day, I shy away from spending time on the phone because of early childhood restrictions. It was a requirement that we all be quiet when he was sleeping. He often slept during the day when he was working nights, so this restriction was important to a family of youngsters.

Replacing Clapboards: Uncle Will was a great carpenter, patient and unerring—to an extent. He had no electric tools, so all carpentry involved significant physical effort. When I was 15, Uncle Will asked me to help out with a particular project: replacing the rotted outside clapboards on one side of the upper floor in the house in Rensselaer. I was enlisted to measure boards so that he could cut them to the proper size. Because of his occasional temper outbursts, I was very apprehensive about doing things right.

By my measurement, we needed one board to be exactly 15 feet long and 11 inches wide. To ensure accuracy, Uncle Will asked me to remeasure. Since the lumber was 12 inches wide, it required Uncle Will to saw off exactly one inch for a length of 15 feet. This he did unerringly with the hand-powered rip saw. When he handed me the finished piece, I put it in place, only to find I had measured wrong and that the replacement board didn't have to be cut at all. I was shaking in my sneakers when I confessed my mistake. Uncle Will's face turned red, and he let out a string of oaths that rang throughout the neighborhood. When he was finished swearing, I was so nervous that I began to laugh—and then, incredibly enough, he did too.

His Politics: In 1932, as the depression worsened, Uncle Will voted for Franklin. D. Roosevelt instead of Herbert Hoover. On his way to the voting polls in 1936, he was stopped by a staunch Republican neighbor and given several well-thought-out reasons for why he should vote against FDR, the main one being that the Democrats were pushing "big government" much too far in the areas of public works, social benefits, labor power, etc. From then on, Uncle Will was so conservative that he was nicknamed the "Red Eagle" by his co-workers. His influence surely "trickled down" into the next generation.

Not only did Uncle Will dislike FDR, he hated Eleanor Roosevelt, who became prominent in her own right. She had a high wavering voice when she spoke. Her medium for communicating was by radio, and for some reason, it seemed that Uncle Will would always tune in on her speeches, making negative comments as she continued with her address.

Every so often, he would shout out, "I don't have to listen to your (expletive)," get up out of his chair, walk over to the radio, and snap it off. However, in a few moments, he would turn the radio back on, resume listening to Eleanor, swear some more, and once again snap off the radio. This would happen four or five times during one speech. It was interesting to witness this process on a regular basis.

The night President Roosevelt died in Warm Springs, Georgia, the phone rang and rang with different people calling in to give Uncle Will the "good" news.

His Cooking: Uncle Will was a terrible cook, but he insisted on preparing breakfast for anyone entering the kitchen in the morning. He would light the gas burner and put on the skillet. Then in one fell swoop he would crack an egg, drop it in the pan, scoop it up with a spatula, and dump it on a plate, practically raw and very runny. Those who witnessed this routine would avoid the kitchen in the morning.

In 1955, Uncle Will died at the age of 67. My main regret was that I just wasn't mature enough to tell him how much I loved him and how much we all appreciated what he had done for our family in providing us with a home, putting food on the table, and doling out liberal portions of care and love over the years.

Aunt Bessie was the maiden aunt who unhesitatingly stepped into the responsibility of helping to manage our large family. She quit her job as a secretary in a department store so that she could help her sister, who did home care and house cleaning, bring up the children.

Aunt Bessie had such an optimistic outlook that it was contagious. She had a knack for keeping us occupied, particularly on those dull, cold, winter days when we were confined to the house with little initiative to do anything but bicker. She would play games with us, endless hours of Parcheesi, Chinese checkers, card games, and pick-up-sticks. She would tell fascinating stories of her experiences, even though she hadn't traveled much.

The Spaghetti Dinner: One of my favorites of the often-repeated experiences she described was the time she went to an Italian restaurant with her friend, Alice Goey. When Alice stuck her fork into the spaghetti, it hit something hard—which turned out to be a set of false teeth!

Gekko: She had an amazing imagination. During the warm weather months, she would often produce from out of nowhere a little, grey, furry, toy monkey that she named Gekko. She would talk to the monkey and have him talk to us in ventriloquist-like fashion. In the winter, Gekko would disappear. When we asked his whereabouts, Aunt Bessie would say, "Gekkie's gone south to Florida." And we believed her!

She wasn't happy, however, on the day brother Bleecker found the toy monkey hidden under clothing in a bureau drawer. He boldly showed Gekko to Aunt Bessie, and she promptly whacked him with a wooden coat hanger. She was a loving woman but also very strict.

The Afternoon Nap Incident: Bleecker and I were the youngest of the children and as such were required to take naps in the afternoon when we were home up until the age of 10. We slept together in a large bedroom accommodating five of us. Aunt Bessie would get us into bed, pull down the window shade to make it dark, and then exit by slowly closing the door when she was sure we were on our way to dreamland. As we got older, instead of going right to sleep, Bleek and I would wait until the door was closed and then begin animated conversations about anything that came into our mind. For some time we even invented a running serial-type conversation based on "The Phantom," a comic-strip action character we saw in the Sunday newspaper.

Aunt Bessie deftly administers a beating with the dreaded hairbrush.

However, Aunt Bessie put us to bed so that we would go to sleep. There was no nonsense to be going on, which included any type of conversation. It didn't take her long to realize that we would start talking once she left the bedroom. Her favorite implement of discipline was a brown wooden hairbrush with which she would whack us when we were unruly.

One day, the bedroom shades were pulled down and soon afterward, Aunt Bessie silently closed the door. Cunningly, however, she remained in the darkened bedroom with us instead of exiting. As usual, Bleek and I waited a few minutes and then started up our naptime conversation. Suddenly, Aunt Bessie loomed out of the darkness with the dreaded hairbrush in her hand. I was the closest to her, so I was the target. I began to whimper, fearing the blow.

She demanded, "Are you going to cry?" To which I responded, "Yes!" She raised the brush higher and once again asked, "Are you going to cry?" Again I responded, "Yes!" This was obviously not the response she was looking for, because the brush was raised even further, wavering in her hand, ready to come crashing down upon me. Once more the question, "Are you going to cry?"

This time around, I saw the light. "No, Aunt Bessie, please don't hit me!" With that she snarled, "Then go to sleep right now or I'll be back with the hairbrush!" She walked out of the room and closed the door behind her. It was several days before Bleek and I worked up the courage to resume our serial conversations about "The Phantom," but we were very careful to make sure no one else was in the darkened room.

The Oaken Wash Stick: In addition to the brown wooden hairbrush, Aunt Bessie often threatened us with another weapon of mass destruction: a heavy, bleached, oaken wash stick that she used to stir laundry in the wash tub. I don't recall her ever using it (if she did we would have been bruised for life), but the mere threat was enough to produce instant behavior.

The Castleton Bus Incident: When brother Larry was in grade school, he was scheduled to attend the annual school boat trip for a picnic on the Hudson. How the children would all look forward to that event: a full day riding to Kingston on the Day Liner, enjoying a picnic in the park, and then returning to Albany on a different Day Line boat coming north from New York City. Unfortunately, young Larry had made a sassy remark to Aunt Bessie. She threatened to cancel his picnic plans and put him instead on the Castleton bus that would take him to Hoogebergh.

Unfortunately, Larry didn't know Aunt Bessie was bluffing as she escorted him to the bus stop. While at the stop, a classmate walked up and asked Larry, "Aren't you going on the class picnic?" He answered, jerking his thumb toward Aunt Bessie, "I was, but this damned fool won't let me." That did it. When the bus arrived, Aunt Bessie pushed Larry through the door with the instructions to the driver, "Take this boy to Staats Island and don't let him off until he gets there." Off went the bus, along with Larry's shattered hopes of attending the picnic.

The Peace Offering of Candy: When brother Barry was in his senior year of high school, he committed an indiscretion: he mysteriously failed to come home one night. There was an unconfirmed rumor that he had had a dalliance with a young neighborhood lady of questionable reputation. We never did find out the true details. Aunt Bessie felt disgraced and wouldn't speak to Barry for days. One evening, he came home from work with a peace offering—a box of chocolate candy—and Aunt Bessie loved chocolate. Unfortunately, he selected the cheapest brand. When she opened the gift-wrapped box and looked at the label, she snarled, "Schraft's," opened the upstairs bedroom window, and threw it into the night. So much for the peace offering.

A Twisted Sense of Humor: Sometimes, Aunt Bessie exhibited a twisted sense of humor. For instance, when I was in Miss Reilly's sixth grade class (the lady couldn't have been more Irish), Aunt Bessie handed me an orange sweatshirt to wear to school on St. Patrick's Day. It was like waving a red flag in front of a bull, and I had no idea what incurred her wrath. She promptly sent me home to change my shirt. Aunt Bess (of Scot-Northern Ireland descent) thought that was grand fun.

Playing Bridge, Darts, and Acting: On cold-weather evenings, Aunt Bessie would play bridge with the neighbor ladies one night a week. By the time she got home, we would all be in bed, but we were awakened by her fascinating recapping of the excitement at the bridge table. "Sarah was a sly fox," she would report, "holding that trump until the last minute!" or "We gave Anna Rikon a present for her birthday which was a roll of toilet paper with a note 'A friend in need is a friend indeed.' She didn't think it was funny." She also joined the ladies in a dart league at the local church. Once in a while, the church ladies would put on a play for the neighbors in the city blocks closest to the church. I can clearly recall her playing the role of Snow White and coughing up the chunk of poisoned apple she had swallowed.

In 1943, Aunt Bessie died from heart problems when in her early 60s. The family lost a legendary, good-hearted disciplinarian whose main legacy was hundreds of wonderful memories.

Good Friend Wil

Wil Koveleskie became a part of the extended family at the ripe old age of eight. He befriended brother Barry in grade school and never left the scene until he passed on at age 77. In the meantime, he exemplified the concept of a good friend. It seemed he was always dependable, in good humor and somewhat grouchy at the same time. When brother Barry transferred with his job to New Jersey, we retained Wil, and our relationship became even closer as the years passed.

If there was a car breakdown in the wee hours of a winter night, Wil was the one to call. If someone was needed to help buzz saw through a winter supply of wood, Wil was there. He was a good natured worker bee, to be sure. He had an uncanny knack for solving problems when the solution wasn't obvious. Wil was also quick to criticize (in a friendly way) and prone to razz friends and family for shortcomings.

My favorite recollection of Wil was the time he was razzing brother Barry about his wartime Navy experiences. Barry had been stationed in Texas as a Yeoman (office worker) while Wil had traveled considerably in the North Atlantic, serving in the Armed Guard (Navy personnel on board protecting merchant ships carrying supplies to Europe). Wil had been to England, Scotland, and even Murmansk in Russia. He had seen a lot of action.

In one post-war conversation, Wil needled Barry when a group of us gathered for small talk. "Barry," he said, "while you were sitting on your butt at a desk in Texas, I was fighting the war in the North Atlantic. Do you know I crossed the Arctic Circle *five* times?" Brother Barry was quick to respond, "Wil, if you say you crossed the Arctic Circle five times, that means you are still up there!" That response brought down the house and has been a favorite recollection of so many of us over the years.

Brother Bleecker

My next older brother, Bleecker, was a lifelong friend. He was truly eclectic with deep interests. In his youth, it was tropical fish, dinosaurs, and volcanoes; in his adult years, it was his family, classical music, birds, and hiking in the Catskills. In fact, he climbed the 35 high peaks (over 3500 feet) in the Catskills. Later he had a heart attack and then a four-artery bypass. Following that, he climbed the 35 peaks once again!

In his formative years, however, he was just plain obstreperous. He had an unnerving way of knowing just how to push people's buttons to the point of driving them over the edge. He grew out of it, but in the interim, it was rough going.

In my pre-teens, I was prone to temper tantrums. Couple that tendency with an older brother who knew how to incite extreme reactions, and there was a "perfect storm" of confrontation.

The Jelly Beans: When we were very young, Uncle Will used to generously give the younger children 25 cents a month as an allowance. At that age, I aped just about everything Bleecker did when it came to blowing the money to the wind. One time, Bleek went into the local penny candy store as I waited for him outside. When he came out he had a good sized bag of jelly beans. I asked him how much of his allowance he spent, and he told me all of it. So I merrily followed his footsteps into the store and ordered 25 cents worth of jelly beans. In those days, that amount of money went a long way, and the proprietor gave me a sack of candy so bulky and heavy that I could barely carry it. When I met brother Bleek outside, he looked at my bag and dissolved into peels of mirth, telling me that he really had spent only a nickel. Naturally, I burst into tears. Bleek still had 20 cents to spend, and I was broke for a month.

The Block of Wood: At this point in time, I can't recall the reason for the confrontation, but once again, brother Bleek had driven me to the brink of a tantrum. We were in the kitchen together at the time, alone in the house. Infuriated, I seized a good-sized block of firewood and chased Bleek out of the kitchen. He ran through the living room and then into the poolroom hall. With all the effort that could be mustered, I threw the block of wood at him. Suddenly, there was a groan and a muffled voice moaning, "I think my leg is broken."

With that, I was immediately contrite. "Bleek," I shouted, "I didn't mean to hurt you!" I ran through the living room and into the pool room hall. It turned out to be a ruse. The block of wood had missed Bleek, so he grabbed it, took a few steps up the pool room hallway stairs, and awaited me. As I passed through the door into the hallway, he brought the block of wood down full force on my shoulders. The blow was so powerful that I was knocked flat onto the hallway floor.

The Veery Bird: As an adult, Bleek was so enthusiastic about hiking in the Catskills that it was contagious. He even organized a group called "Bleecker's Creepers" an older group of people who hiked diligently, but somewhat slowly at every season of the year. I resisted Bleek's continuous requests to join him in a hike, but finally I gave in just to shut him up. On a frosty morning, we began the ascent up North Mountain. It soon became grueling. Without Bleek, I would have been hopelessly lost after traveling a few miles into the thicket, even though the trails were well marked. The fact is that I can get lost in my own driveway at home.

In addition to the hiking, Bleek had a variety of other interests. He seemed to know every plant, tree, and flower along the way. "See that flower, Bill; that's a jack-in-the-pulpit." He treated me as if I was some youngster on Sesame Street. He plucked a flower and bought it close to my face. "Now that little thing standing up is `jack' and the other thing is his pulpit." More Sesame Street. I didn't dare admit that it was most interesting.

As a bird watcher, Bleek had a wealth of knowledge about our winged friends all along the trail. Thrushes, sparrows, finches, warblers. He could even imitate their bird calls and had coerced me into borrowing a CD that featured bird calls. I confess that I listened with interest but would be damned to let him know that. Assuming I had memorized the calls, he pointed to a feathered friend and announced that it was a veery bird. The bird, I remembered, had a call similar to the sound of its name, Veer-y, which sounded somewhat like a downward spiral.

"Now, Bill, I want you to make the sound of the veery bird," he said. "In the middle of the woods? Here and now?" I inquired incredulously. "Here and now, Bill...NOW!" He could be quite forceful. Stubbornly I resisted. "Bleecker, I'm now 57 years old, and I have no intention of imitating the call of a veery bird." "Then, Bill, I will disappear into the underbrush and bushwhack my way home. You, of course, will be hopelessly lost and wander around for days." The prospect of his prediction rang true, and so, like a mimic, I stood there in the middle of nowhere calling out "Veer-y, veer-y, veer-y" in a downward spiral until he was satisfied.

At the end of the trail, a huge sigh of relief emerged from my lungs. No more hiking, no more fearing getting lost, no more trees, wild flowers, or damned birds. That was it for me until the next time he talked me into a hike "to see the frost" but that's another story.

It's a little hard to believe, but after so many years of quarreling, Bleek and I became fast friends. He died at the age of 65 from prostate cancer. His passing left a real void. In his later years and during his terminal illness, we had spent as many hours as possible together.

The 1931 Model A Ford Roadster—the Inanimate Family Member

It all started in 1931 when she was manufactured in Dearborn, Michigan. For several years she was transferred to various owners, and in the mid-1930s she was bought by Mr. Keyer, the Dutch-born handyman who lived next door to Hoogebergh. Unfortunately, Mr. Keyer enjoyed his liquid refreshments, and even 70 years ago, drinking and driving didn't mix. After a few fender benders, the police asked Mr. Keyer to make a decision: either stop driving or stop drinking. He chose the former and continued to imbibe until his drinking finally killed him at the age of 89!

In 1937, he sold the jaunty, ensign-blue Model A Ford Roadster for the tidy sum of $75 to Mother, who drove it for several years. It was one fine-looking vehicle. It had a spare tire mounted on each front fender. Cowl lights, used for parking lights, identified it as a "deluxe" roadster. It had a canvas top (which cost $75 in 1950 and has been replaced periodically by me, most recently at a cost of $450!) and a rumble seat.

If the car had been human, Mother could have been convicted of child abuse. Her driving was atrocious. She usually started off in second gear. She dented every fender, several times. She was prone to cut off other vehicles in traffic. As a passenger with her, I can clearly recall hearing an exasperated driver shout, "If you can't drive it, park it, grandma!" as she found her way through traffic in downtown Albany.

The Model A was often used as a work vehicle. With the rumble seat open, it could carry two railroad ties horizontally across the back of the car. The heavy ties were sawed up to stock the wood pile for winter. To use the buzz saw, the rear wheel of the Model A was jacked up, and the leather belt connected to the saw platform was attached. After that, the car was started up and put in gear. As the raised rear wheel spun, it activated the axle to which the saw was attached, and the whirring sound of the buzz saw would begin.

One time in the late 1930s when we were collecting abandoned railroad ties from the shoulder of the track, a number of us were involved in the heavy lifting job. There were several teenagers, brother Larry, and Uncle Will (then considered an old guy in his 50s). It was sheer delight to the youngsters when, in loading a tie onto the Model A, one end bounced up and caught Uncle Will under his jaw, causing his mouth to open, and his false teeth to fly out. Fortunately, he wasn't injured, but it sure created a memorable moment.

As the family grew older, we became larger in more than one way. We would often have a few friends as guests. On the usual Sunday night routine of driving to Rensselaer in the Model A so that we could go to school during the week, there might be as many as 11 passengers riding in (and on) the car—one on each front fender, three in the front seat, two in the rumble seat, one on each rear fender, and two standing on the carrier behind the rumble seat. Obviously, this was in the days before strict safety regulations.

I vividly recall the time the Model A stalled as we were crossing the railroad tracks near Hoogebergh. There were several people in the car, one of whom was most upset at the prospect of being hit by a train. Mother got the car running and backed off the tracks to avoid the oncoming train. In the process, she turned the wheel too sharply and the roadster began to slide down the embankment leading up to the tracks. The squeamish young man shouted, "I'm gonna get the hell out!" to which my mother fired back, "then get the hell out!" Somehow she managed to overcome the backward slide and get us back on the road.

The Model A often seemed to have a personality of its own. When cantankerous, it would stall or just plain wouldn't start and had to be cranked by hand, a back-breaking procedure for those who recall the experience. When affable, it would purr along at a cruising speed of 35 mph. It was never a smooth ride, and just managing the steering was a Herculean task when compared with driving a vehicle with power steering.

Sister Jane had a turn at the wheel when first learning to drive. She steered the car off the main highway onto the dirt road leading into Hoogebergh. Unfortunately, she didn't turn sharply enough and proceeded to drive into the swampy area just south of the road. Somehow, Jane never lost her cool (as did the passengers) and managed to get the car back on the dirt road. I believe that was her sole experience of driving the roadster.

Brother Larry often drove the car to high school. He sometimes used it for sight gags. He had made a straw-filled dummy, complete with old fedora hat, and would have it riding in the rumble seat. At other times, he would stuff the dummy into the rumble seat and close it so that just a leg and a shoe protruded.

The Ford is a survivor. During the World War II years, brother Barry frequently drove the Model A to high school events. On one frigid winter night, he and a buddy drove the car to a high school basketball game in Castleton. It was so cold the radiator froze and boiled over at a location far removed from the city. They had to stop at a frozen-over stream and break the ice to get water to replace what had boiled away. Of course, the radiator had to be drained before leaving the car for the night.

When brother Larry came out of the Navy after World War II, Mother turned the keys over to him. For a few years, he drove it daily from Rensselaer to Schenectady to commute to work at his job with General Electric. What a fun experience that was in wintertime. It was a roadster, a convertible, an open car that required celluloid side curtains in the cold months. The curtains, however, merely shielded the wind. They did not do much for the inside temperature. There was a manifold heater that brought a blast of heat from the exhaust manifold through a small hole into the Ford's cabin. It was hot enough to melt the soles of your shoes, but that was it. The rest of your body would be rigid with cold.

Larry was a fine mechanic and kept the car in good shape. In the days before interstate highways, he drove winding country roads to skiing slopes in Vermont some 60 miles from home.

Larry transferred the roadster to me in the late '40s when he bought a more modern vehicle. It has remained in my possession, licensed and driven even as this book is being written in 2010. It demands respect because it is one year older than I am.

My first driving experience was at the wheel of our Model A at the ripe old age of 14. Brother Larry and I were taking the rustic route to Hoogebergh, traveling a dirt road that pretty much paralleled the Hudson River. Unexpectedly he said, "I think it's about time you learned to drive, and before I knew it, I was sitting behind the wheel. It was not a pretty experience. Jostling and jolting along, trying to get the hang of it, I proceeded to cross a railroad spur and managed to drive down the railroad tracks instead of crossing them on the road. We bumped along what seemed to be an endless succession of railroad ties before braking. We both heaved a sigh of relief, and brother Larry once again took over the wheel.

In 1949, I was a high school senior and old enough to drive the car to school daily. There were some fun experiences. There was the time my buddy Beaky and I were driving home from a basketball game and ran out of gas. Fortunately we were on a bridge over the railroad and could coast all the way to the nearest Mobil station. In 1949, gas was 35 cents a gallon. The tank was bone dry and so were our finances. Between the two of us, we mustered up 17 cents and persuaded the attendant to put in a half gallon, just enough to get us home several blocks away.

In the spring of 1950, Beaky and I decided on a real adventure. In late March, we took off for Cape Cod in the Model A. With no superhighways and our cruising speed of 35 mph, it took more than 12 hours on a trip that today would take less than 3 hours. Of course, we had a flat tire along the way. Of course we got stopped by the police. At that time cars didn't have to be inspected, and I had let the brakes deteriorate to the point where they were practically useless.

On an earlier occasion, a cop put his foot down on the brake and it went nonstop to the floorboard. "I thought my foot was on the clutch," he admonished, but he declined to give a citation.

The 1931 Model A Ford Deluxe Roadster

When the police stopped us on the way to Cape Cod, we had perfected a ruse. Since the foot brake didn't work, Beak would grab the emergency brake, which worked much better. The police never knew about our ploy. Not only that, they were keenly interested in the car's novelty accessory: a tugboat bell that brother Larry had installed when he was in high school. It had been "removed" from an abandoned tugboat in Kingston, NY, and mounted on the wall of the rumble seat in the Model A. He rigged a wire that enabled the driver to clang the bell from his position behind the steering wheel. It was quite a sensation for the young ladies and the envy of the guys, and it fascinated the state police who had stopped us on the way to Cape Cod. One cop said, "Let me hear it again" after we had demonstrated the novelty. We could easily have spent the night in jail, but instead were ushered on our way by admiring officers.

After all the tedious driving on a very chilly March night, we finally arrived at Cape Cod in the area of Dennisport. We had very little money and no place to stay. Friends that Beaky had hoped to locate were out of town. Undaunted, we found a summer tourist cabin with a window that could be lifted open. Inside we crawled. Of course, the cabin was cold. The two of us huddled in a bed shivering through the night with only our overcoats and clothing for protection.

The next morning, we strolled along the beach, and by the time we got back to the cabin, the local police were standing next to the Model A. They told us a neighbor had called about the suspicious intruders in the old car and that they had come to investigate. We had to confess our situation. After listening to our story, one of the policemen said, "Fellows, we won't put you in jail if you just drive off the Cape by noon." That was the end of our senior-year traveling adventure.

There was also that memorable day when neighbor Joe Podoba and I were casually driving south on Rte. 9J en route to Hoogebergh. Suddenly there was the distinct sound of something dragging on the pavement. We stopped the car and peered underneath. Sure enough, the muffler had broken loose and was dragging on the road. It was extremely hot, since the engine had been running for some time. What to do? There wasn't any wire in the car to tie the muffler up so it wouldn't drag on the road. Joe offered his newly purchased belt. We strapped the belt around the muffler and to the frame of the car, started it up, and proceeded on our way—for about 100 feet when the dragging reoccurred. Sure enough, the hot muffler had burned right through Joe's new belt. He took it good naturedly.

Then there was the time when I felt the Model A needed an extreme makeover. With limited finances, I bought bright purple (my favorite color) paint at Kresge's (now Kmart) for $1 a pint and painted it on with a cheap brush. The finish was awful but the color was startling—for a few weeks. Then the sun faded the cheap paint, and it turned to a sickening pale blue. A better paint job later on made a big difference.

There were other adventurous journeys in the Model A. When sister Jane and her family moved to Buffalo, some 350 miles west of Hoogebergh, we would drive there, taking more than 10 hours each way on Route 20. On one trip, we had three flat tires. Since there were only two spare tires on the front fenders, it meant getting one repaired before proceeding on.

As a high school graduation present, brother Larry and his buddy Carl replaced the engine with a rebuilt one and included in the gift wheel drums with a hydraulic brake setup. That was a most-needed improvement. The earlier mechanical brakes were totally undependable, and it required at least a city block of space before the car would stop.

On a balmy autumn afternoon, my friend Betty and I were driving down the hill of State Street, the main street in Albany, on our way home from college. It was 5 p.m. and the traffic was bustling—crowds crossing the street and cars everywhere as the rush hour was in full swing. At the main intersection, a car came to a sudden stop, and I knew the mechanical brakes wouldn't allow the Model A to stop in time. We slowed but still crashed into the rear bumper of the stopped car. The sound was deafening. Heads turned; other vehicles stopped. Embarrassing! For me, it was just a matter of time before the police would arrive and I'd lose my driver's license. But that was not to be. The lady driving the car that had stopped ahead of me jumped out of the front seat and came running back to me."I'm so sorry I stopped so suddenly," she said. "I hope you aren't too upset!" Upset? I was ecstatic! Betty and I proceeded on our way home.

In my early college years, the roadster continued to be my main source of transportation. I can recall the disappointment on my date's face when I showed up in the Model A roadster to take her to the college prom. For some reason, grease on her white hoop skirt didn't go over well.

Eventually, time took its toll. In early 1952, the main bearing in the engine gave out, and it was time to retire the Model A. Sadly I parked it in a secluded area at Hoogebergh and not long after, joined the Navy for a two-year stint. I bought another car and sadly watched as rust began to disintegrate the family jewel.

In 1964, attitudes and circumstances changed. The awakening came the day brother Bleek used the rumble seat lid for pistol practice. At that point, it was time to take the Model A to the dump or to renovate it. The renovation took a couple of years. So much paint removal. Yet another rebuilt engine. A new canvas top. New tires. A paint job. Soon she was looking very spiffy.

From then on, the Model A Ford became my auxiliary transportation. I drove it daily to work at the college for two decades in fall, winter, and spring. Plexiglass window panes replaced the side curtains, but they still didn't keep the car warm.

On one frigid winter afternoon, I picked up one of my hitchhiking students on his way home from the college. The young man's teeth chattered as he huddled in the front seat. "Aren't you cold, Mr. Staats?" he asked. Applying a little humor, I responded, "Mr. Summers, you must realize that cold is a relative thing. If we were in Alaska, for instance, you would probably think that today's temperatures were moderate." He nodded courteously and couldn't wait to get out when his stop came.

I am still getting used to some perplexing, nonsensical remarks and questions regarding the Model A now that she is an antique and still on the road. The most common question is "Are you still driving that car?" This is when the car is stopped but still running. The inclination is to come forth with a rejoinder such as "Oh, no, I tie a rope to my waist and pull it wherever I'm going!"

One time I was having carburetor problems and decided to repair it in a Kmart parking lot. It was a mid-summer hot and humid afternoon. I took the carburetor off, disassembled it, and was busy cleaning the inner parts, when a curious bystander asked, "Are you having some trouble with the car?" Here I am sitting on the running board on a hot summer day, fiddling with parts and I get that inane question. However, I did not verbalize my considered response, "Oh, no, I just love to sit here and play with car parts in this parking lot when there isn't much else going on."

There have been many similar ridiculous comments. Too many to write about. My favorite was the time I pulled into a gas station during a February snowstorm. Another customer poked his head in the cabin and asked, "Do you drive this car in the winter?"

After 1985, common sense finally set in. From then on, the car has been driven only in the warm-weather months. It becomes more and more of a chore as age creeps in and patience and capabilities diminish, but who could abandon an old friend?

When daughter Giss married in the late 1980s, she wanted to leave the wedding in the rumble seat with her new husband. Gussying up the roadster was a much-needed activity by this time. The car was sanded and dents re-paired and a brand new coat of expensive maroon paint was sprayed on by Tim, a friend of nephew Pieter who requested as pay only a carton of cigarettes and two six packs of beer each day he worked. When it was completed, Tim wasn't in good shape but the Model A looked magnificent. Silver paint replaced the previous yellow on the spoke wheels.

The 1931 Model A Ford Roadster has been willed to my most mechanically talented son, Grant, with the proviso that it remain in its original state and not be modified. When I informed him of the bequest, the young man's response (with a glint in his eye) was, "Since you're leaving the car to me, I suggest you start taking better care of it!"

CHAPTER IX
FAMILY LINEAGE FROM 1600 TO 2009

Mrs. Barent (Connie) Staats made very thorough genealogy studies in the 1960s through the 1990s. In this listing, I include (in addition to the two generations that preceded the building of Hoogebergh) only the few owners of Hoogebergh rather than all the Staats descendents who are now scattered across the United States of America:

Generation 1—**Major Abraham Staats**: In the first chapter of this book is a document that explains the origin of the Staats name. Admiral Ghyse was a Dutch naval hero who was responsible for defeating part of the Spanish fleet. Thus the Staats name started in the Netherlands sometime before the turn of the 16th century. Abraham was born in Holland in 1617 and died in America in 1694. He migrated to America in 1642, sailing on the Dutch ship *Houttuyn*. He was a surgeon and fur trader. Major Abraham returned to the Netherlands in 1664 when the English overthrew the Dutch and named the colony New York, replacing the Dutch name, New Netherland. Abraham stayed in Holland seven years and then returned to America. He married Catryna Jochems. His home, which has been considerably remodeled, is in the town of Stockport, north of Hudson in Columbia County.

Generation 2—**Joachim Staats (1654-1712):** He was the son of Major Abraham who first occupied Hoogebergh when it was sold to him by Killaen Van Rensselaer in 1696. Joachim married Anna Borrent. Their names are clearly etched on a brownstone grave marker in the Hoogeberg cemetery located on the top of the knoll. He was a trader, sloop owner, and attorney. Joachim was active in politics and became involved in the Leisler uprising, which supported the accession of William and Mary of Orange, from Holland, to the throne of England. He was placed in control of the garrison at the Albany fort. (Shirley Dunn, "Settlement Patterns in Rensselaerwick" *de Halve Maen Magazine*, 1995, p. 20.)

Generation 3—**Barent Staats (1680-1752):** Joachim's son had a house in the city of Albany with his wife, Neeltje Vandenbergh, whom he married in 1701. When his father became ill, Barent and Neeltje moved to Hoogebergh, but they retained their Albany home and divided their time between the two houses. Barent and Neeltje's names appear on the same gravestone as that of his father, Joachim.

Generation 4—**Joachim Staats (1717-1804):** Joachim and his brother, Gerritt, inherited Hoogebergh from their father, Barent. Joachim married Elizabeth Schuyler. In 1752, after their father's death, the two brothers divided the Hoogebergh property into four sections. Gerritt Staats built a house on the north side of the Hoogebergh knoll. This property was later sold out of the Staats family.

Generation 5—**Colonel Philip Staats (1754-1814):** He was Joachim Staats' son and married Anna VanAlstyne. He was injured in the Revolutionary War. It was Colonel Philip who is purported to have received a visit from General George Washington at Hoogebergh in 1782.

Generation 6—**Joachim Staats (1793-1866):** He inherited Hoogebergh from his father, Colonel Philip Staats. He married Catherine Breese, who lived nearby on the river road that is now Route 9J.

Joachim Peter Staats (1793-1866)

Catherine Breese Staats (1798-1861)

Lawrence Anthony Staats

Generation 7—**Lawrence Anthony Staats (1843 1921)**: He inherited Hoogebergh from Joachim Staats. He became involved in two businesses: operating a feed store in the city of Rensselaer and being a partner in the operation of an ice house on the Hoogebergh premises. He spent considerable time in New York City, renting an apartment there. His purpose in going to the big city was to procure customers for the upstate businesses he partnered in. Lawrence Anthony married Jennie Ostrum, a woman with artistic talent from New Jersey. She did not at all enjoy country living at Hoogebergh and spent as little time there as possible. Lawrence and Jennie had two children, Mabel and Lawrence Arthur. Jennie Ostrum Staats is buried in New Jersey, and Lawrence Anthony is buried in an unmarked grave in the Hoogebergh cemetery.

Generation 8—**Lawrence Arthur Staats (1881-1932)**: He married Esther Smith of Rensselaer. Lawrence (my father) lived at Hoogebergh and worked as a clerk in the Staats family feed store in Rensselaer. He was very much an outdoors-man and thoroughly enjoyed hunting as well as sailing on the Hudson. "Arthur" as he was called, was a bachelor until age 37. He and Esther had seven children—one girl followed by six boys. He died from a blood clot at the young age of 51.

Lawrence Arthur Staats

Esther Smith Staats

Generation 9–**Lawrence Arthur Staats (1923-2008)**: When our father, Arthur, died, Arthur's share of Hoogebergh went to his wife, Esther. Brother "Larry," as he was commonly called, together with our brother Joachim, was instrumental in consolidating the ownership of Hoogebergh within the direct lineage of our father, Arthur, by buying out the descendents of three cousins. He graduated from Worcester Polytechnic Institute with a degree in mechanical engineering and spent most of his life sailing as an engineering officer on merchant marine vessels. At age 56, he married Torill Kaamsvaag, a young Norwegian shipping clerk whom he met while his ship was docked in Alesund, Norway. They had two daughters, Monica and Ingrid.

Generations 10 and 11–1992 to 2008*:* Hoogebergh is now incorporated with ownership shares distributed among most members of the Staats family in the direct lineage of Lawrence Arthur Staats and his wife, Esther. When the corporation was formed, five of the seven children of Lawrence and Esther Staats (and their spouses) were the original shareholders. The two children who did not participate in ownership are Garret, who died in an accident at age 5, and Joachim, who sold his one-half ownership in Hoogebergh to other family members in 1982.

The ninth and tenth generation shares are owned as follows (there are no shares yet held by members of the eleventh generation):

- Elizabeth Jane's (1921-1977) shares were transferred to her husband, Hans Dirzuweit, who transferred some of his shares to his two children, Tientje Willis and Hans Staats Dirzuweit of the tenth generation. The eleventh-generation member from this family is Daniel Dirzuweit.
- Lawrence Arthur's (1923-2008) shares were transferred to his wife, Torill, and also to his daughters, Monica and Ingrid of the tenth generation.
- Barent Staats (1925-present) and his wife, Connie, have transferred some of their shares to their children: Kim Lucas, Cheryl Staats, and Randal Staats of the tenth generation. The eleventh generation of this family are Emily and Barry Staats and Garrett Wininger.
- Bleecker Staats (1929-1994) and his wife, Doris (deceased in 1992), bequeathed their shares to their offspring of the tenth generation: Maelene Dapson, Charles Staats, Pieter Staats, and Amanda Traudt. The eleventh generation includes Emily, Abigail, Joshua, and David Staats; Nathaniel and Lucas Staats; and Schuyler, Miranda, Kristina, Agatha, and Eleanor Traudt.
- William Staats (me, 1932-present) and my wife, Sandra (deceased 2005), distributed most of our shares to our seven children: Mark, Grant, Jennifer Hoeffner, Kristina Erby, Heather Waters, Greg, and Victoria of the tenth generation. The eleventh generation includes Meghan and Kevin Staats, Ethan and Evan Staats, Zachary and Nicholas Hoeffner, Matthew and Brandon Erby, and Tyler, Sawyer, Connor, and Hannah Waters.

Hoogebergh Shareholders—Spring, 2009

Top Row (l to r): Hans Dirzuweit, William Staats, Torill Staats, Barent Staats
Middle Row (l ro r) Monica Staats, Ingrid Staats, Amanda Staats Traudt, Kristina Staats
    Erby,   Heather Staats Waters, Cheryl Staats, Victoria Staats, Jennifer Staats Hoeffner
Bottom Row (l ro r) Pieter Van Wie Staats, Grant Staats, Mark Staats, Greg Staats, Randal
    Staats

Missing from Photo: Constance Staats, Hans Staats Dirzuweit, Charles Staats, Maelene
    Staats Dapson, Kim Staats Lucas, Tientje Staats Willis

APPENDIX
RECOLLECTIONS FROM FRIENDS AND FAMILY

It was suggested to me that some written recollections of friends and family over the years would add to the nostalgia of the work. Some of these sentiments have been abridged. Here are some of the recollections:

I remember stomping through the cornfields...riding in the doodlebug and being afraid of wild dogs...walking to the south end of the island to throw bottles at a big concrete piling. I didn't have much of an arm, but the smashing was deeply satisfying.
— Katie Fallon, social service worker, Portland, Oregon

I remember sleigh riding in winter. It was so much fun. My father decided to ride down the hill when there was a coating of ice on the snow. He flew over a jump and landed on his face. After a trip to the hospital and dozens of stitches, he had to face his co-workers the next day and explain how he got hurt.
—Kathy Van Dyke, 50, executive assistant, New York State Dormitory Authority

I recollect viewing the family cemetery, swimming in the Hudson, seeing the colorful autumn leaves, marveling at the way in which family members worked to keep up with the maintenance of a valuable part of history.
— Jim Dyall, retired accounting department assistant chairman, Royal Melbourne Institute of Technology, Melbourne, Australia

I first saw the Staats homestead at a party given by Connie Staats. I remember driving down the dirt road and coming around a bend to see the old house complete with family cemetery on a hill overlooking the river and thinking "How cool!" A trip to Staats Island is like a step back in time. Any given Sunday will find the family swimming, boating, playing croquet, and enjoying each other's company. People bring food, dinners are shared, and friends and visitors are welcome.
—Leah Hoey, New York State Teachers' Retirement System

I love the island. It is where I grew up and is the most familiar thing that I know in my life. When I was away at college, I realized how much I missed the smell of the house and even the smell of the river...so wonderfully comforting. The island is family...is refuge...is home.

— Victoria Staats, secondary school math teacher, tenth-generation shareholder

The homestead evokes pleasant memories of cornfields, the railroad crossing, driving the Model A Ford at age 17, the oogah horn, the beamed ceilings, the curved closet door, the pool table, good food and conversation...and a lovely view of the Hudson.

— Dan Thompson, 62, retired database administrator, Texas Instruments

The first time I bicycled to the "Staats place on the river," it was to hunt, swim, and just hang out with Larry Staats. Many visits followed. We would wave to the day boat and the night boat passing on their way to New York City or Albany. My last glimpse for some years of the homestead came as the train took me past on the way to Fort Dix and World War II-just as a beautiful pheasant glided from the tracks to a patch of sumac.

— Howie Lout, 86, World War II paratrooper, retired college administrator

As Hudson River sailors, neighbors, and friends of the Staats family, we have often observed that the grounds surrounding the old homestead are alive with young and old alike. What a pleasure to see!

— Bette Jane Saiberlich-Poulos, artist and harpist; Dennis Poulos, Ph.D., former professor and associate dean, Albany Medical College

Turning off the main road on the way to Staats Island meant that we were about to reconnect with a place and a family, both of which promised a warm welcome and good times. We could always count on being regaled with tales of Larry's adventures on the high seas or on Lake George. Additions and improve of the American Revolution. One cannot stand near the homestead and look out at the river without thinking of all those hardy souls who have so carefully tended their heritage for the benefit of family and friends for almost 400 years.

— Etheleen Williams, 83, DAR

I have been coming to Staats Island since I was 15 to be with my best friend, Chip Staats. I always feel like family at Staats Island. It is a beautiful, historic setting. The homestead is something 99.99% of the world's people will never experience

and I count myself blessed to be in the .01%.
— James "Murray" Amrod, 49, swimming pool supply company representative

I met Bill Staats in 1950 when we were both freshmen at Albany State Teachers College. I cherish the memories of "hanging out" at the homestead and of being accepted by his Mom, brothers, and friends. It certainly was a relief from dorm life.

— Ray Call, 77, retired high school biology teacher

Arriving on a mildly warm July 4 in 2007, we were taken by the peaceful setting of the Staats family stone house nestled into a rise overlooking a broad sweeping bend in the majestic Hudson River. As most foreigners regard the US as the epitome of the ultra-modern, it was a genuine pleasure to find a part of older colonial America which predates our nation—Australia's—settled history by 150 years. Hoogebergh reminds us of our very earliest houses built of stone around 1830 in the island state of Tasmania.
— Tom Hogg, retired economist and professor, and Judy Hogg, solicitor (attorney), Melbourne, Australia

In the late 1940s, I became familiar with Staats Island along with several high school friends. In the past 58 years, I have memories of Christmas sing-alongs, walking on the frozen river, swimming, weddings, playing cards, and sleeping overnight by the fireplace.
— Edward LaPlante, 78, retired wood shop teacher, Rensselaer Boys and Girls Club; New York State Dept. of Transportation engineer working on roads, docks, and bridges

One year during the early part of World War II when in high school, we almost made the photo collection on the Post Office wall. Several of us took a boat up to the Port of Albany to find scrap iron. Out of nowhere came the FBI to arrest the dastardly thieves or even possibly Nazi spies. Actually, they just took our names and told us to scram. It always amazed me that none of us wound up in prison.
— George Benkly, 83, retired civil engineer working internationally with Bechtel Corp.

The Staats Christmas party at Hoogebergh had so many people attending that to go from one room to another, one had to go outside and re-enter through the door to the next room. To use the restroom, one went to one of the classiest outhouses we've ever seen—it even had curtains on the windows. At the annual choir picnic, we would sit outside to enjoy the view of the Hudson River and watch an occasional bald eagle fly overhead.

*— **Linda Sweetman, retired two-year college admissions director, and Ed Sweetman, retired mathematics teacher***

The Island is the place where family is, where work is, where fun is, whether swimming, Frisbee, waffle ball, or king of the raft. It is the place for Sunday dinners. Everyone I bring down there says, "Wow, this place is cool," and I'd answer, "Yeah, it's alright." The truth is that I love it there. I love everything about it: being outside, eating with my family, and even working, sometimes. If I were to use one word to describe the Island, I would say "home."

*— **Ethan Staats, 18, eleventh generation, prospective Hartwick College student***

Sledding at Hoogebergh is one of my favorite childhood memories. We would climb the hill up to the cemetery and end up down by the baseball field, navigating around the outhouse along the way. The Staats family would invite us in for hot chocolate and ghost stories in front of the fireplace. Everyone was "Aunt" and "Uncle" back then, and conversation and laughter would fill the room.

*— **Patti Hutchinson Kiefer, Danville, California***

I have fond memories of visiting the Island as a young man. Most memorable is how welcome I was made to feel by the Staats family. Be it a summer barbeque, wedding, softball game, or famous "work party," there was never a shortage of good times and good friends.

*— **Dennis Kiefer, 53, vice president, Siemens Corp., and ex-US Marine***

As a member of First Church in Albany's choir over several decades, I have enjoyed the annual picnic. I enjoyed delicious food and beverages, always ending with a gathering in the parlor singing old favorites accompanied by the host playing the piano. Parts of the homestead are original—a good example of strength and endurance.

*— **Mary Kay McCann, retired choir soprano soloist***

The inviting warmth and love of this wonderful old house and its family have created a nostalgic blend that has given many who first entered the Dutch doors truly a sense of "coming home."

*— **Elizabeth Snyder Shannon, 77, retired banker, Liberty, Missouri***

In our early teens, my sisters and I walked over the frozen river from Van Wies Point to the Staats house. As we reached the homestead, the aroma of cooking met us at the door. Esther Staats was in the homey kitchen making doughnuts̨dipping them in hot oil and then into a bag of powdered sugar. They were so good I can almost smell them now.
—Shirley Snyder Prior, 79, homemaker, mother of six, grandmother to several

My memories of affection for the Island center around the annual choir picnic as folks gathered together to eat, talk, and sing and watch together the sun go down. I also remember the times we spent partying at weddings and birthday parties. It seems to me that the physical evolution of the Island to a piece of land vitally connected to the main land is one clue to the story. I can't imagine a place less like an island than Staats Island. Islands are supposed to be quiet and serene, disconnected and lonely. Perhaps that is so when the crowds leave.

—Rev. Gregg Mast, Ph.D., president, New Brunswick Theological Seminary; pastor for 12 years of First Church in Albany (and who conducted the wedding ceremonies for four of the tenth generation)

From as far back as I can remember, the summer has always been a special time for me. As a child, I spent my days with the Staats family rather than attend day care. Soon I would be exploring, swimming, boating, playing croquet, and at times of sheer exhaustion, napping. This is a place that will always be special to me as will the Staats family.

—Darrell Stark, 37, manager of resort hotels in Naples, Florida

Growing up in Rensselaer was synonymous with knowing the Staats family. It was my husband's and my privilege to know them all from the mid-1940s to the present. Our journey has included all manner of hospitality and carefree times together at the "Homestead" or, as we called it "the Island" along the Hudson River. We cannot wait to read about those things not visible to us who were—quite simply—captivated by these witty, honest, loyal, "tell it like it is," outrageous—some might say eccentric— unassuming, diligent, unpretentious, handsome, patriotic, sometimes religiously devout, generous, fun-loving, artistic, rugged, occasionally naughty, individualistic, but, in all, just wonderful traits.

—Jean Burns, retired field supervisor of student teachers, Sage College; and Jim Burns, retired chief service dispatcher, Niagara Mohawk (utility) Corporation

I remember vividly a summer day in the early 1950s swimming in the river with the usual gang at the time. On this occasion, a blanket of dead ale fish was floating on the river. Of course this didn't deter any of us.

—Evelyn Ray Gubitz, retired lab technician

Whatever the activity—parties, work weekend, holidays, swimming, croquet—it's the people you meet again and again. The common denominator of all the friendships and activities is the place itself. I don't think I've ever seen a place that has so much history and character, and yet it is not a museum. I consider myself to be fortunate and blessed.

—Ben Stowell, 42, woodworker, long-time family friend

I love having fun there with my friends, family, softball, croquet, Frisbee, king of the raft, breakfast on the raft. In my early life, I loved spending time there, but then I started to get annoyed because I was forced to go cold turkey away from video games and TV. In the past few years, I have come to appreciate its symbol of love and community in the family where you see each other once or twice a week which other extended families don't do. We all get to know each other very well. Spending time with my extended family has become a treasure to me.

—Zachary Hoeffner, 18, eleventh generation, cadet, US Air Force Academy

My Dad, Carl Hartnagel, died when I was eleven."Uncles" Larry, Barry, and Bill helped fill the void when he died. Enjoying boats, helping build docks, and other projects provided lessons in hard work and subsequent pleasure in getting a job well done.

—Paul Hartnagel, ex-submariner, computer technician

We remember Staats Island as newlyweds, looking for an apartment and answering an ad that would take us down Rte. 9J to a right turn that led to the river. When we came around that last bend and saw the beautiful house with the red roof, we had no idea our lives would forever be changed. Forty-two years later, those images return. The most vivid pictures from 1966 through 1969 were high-tide oil slicks, the sight and sound of tugs at Christmas, the thud-thud of the engines, rattling of windows and the bright red and green lights, a different way for Santa to visit, but unique to this place, for brief moments seemingly belonging to us, an oasis on the Hudson, a gift, transitory but indelible in our hearts and minds.

—Marty, 67, and Gretchen (66) Fallon, occupants of the north wing, 1966-1969. He is a retired school counselor, and she sold beauty products. They now live in Naples, Florida.

I have many fond memories of spending a lot of my time at Hoogebergh in my childhood and in my teens. Sleigh riding in the winter, swimming in the summer, fresh corn on the cob, homemade ice cream, doodlebug rides, and Uncle Larry.

—Bill Reimann, 52, boater, fisherman, outdoor lover

Now in my mature years, "the Island" has given me a sense of identity. I feel complete ownership, belonging, and responsibility for this place I like to call a sanctuary. My life seems natural here. I can see how I fit in and feel great personal reward for my contributions. I do love this place as I know my forefathers have.
—Grant Staats, 49, commander, US Navy SEALS, tenth-generation shareholder

My memories of Staats Island return to 1948. I remember the beautiful vistas of the Hudson River and barge traffic and the many tugs and the beautiful estate. The canoe trips on the river astonished me by the number of tiny balloons floating on the surface of the Hudson. I now know they had risen from the sewage flowing downstream from Rensselaer. I commented to Bill—being naïve—and he was very polite and did not educate me about the use of contraceptives. The homestead was this fantastic historic house. I particularly remember the misshapen door that was taken from the ship that brought the home owners from the Netherlands. My recent visit reaffirmed my memories. I had always hoped to get back to this idyllic setting. The homestead and the gardens and the lawns are so beautiful. I was able to do this in June (2009). I have been lucky to experience a place ofsuch history and beauty.
—Helen Cashman Velie, teacher, homemaker, Sudbury Massachusetts; 1950 classmate from Van Rensselaer High School

I have been attending the annual choir picnic at Staats Island for almost 30 years. It is one of the highlights of my year, not only because of the fellowship but also because of the spectacular location. The Staats homestead combines natural beauty, fascinating history, and a warmth of family.
—Audrey Ming, choir member, First Church in Albany; retired billing coordinator, Sealy Mattress Company

Once entering the old house, it is as if you are back in the late 1600s. The fireplace, the unique doors, and especially the present-day inhabitants are so welcoming. We feel fortunate to be counted as friends of the Staats family for more than 60 years, enjoying such pastimes as sleigh riding, parties, and enlightening discussions until sunrise.
—Fred Hutchinson, 77, retired computer systems sales representative, long-time employee ofthe New York Telephone Company, and Peg Hutchinson, retired executive assistant, New York State Legislature

My first knowledge of the Staats House came from 7th grade students Joe Podoba and Peter Jones (son of Dr. Louis Jones), in social studies, which I taught at Columbia High School. I was urged to plan a visit for members of the Yorker Club. So a bus trip was scheduled and duly came to pass. Pictures were taken by Vice Principal Don Benedict,

who accompanied the expedition. Of course, Spooks of the Valley *by Dr. Louis C. Jones was required reading for 7th grade classes. Later visits were with the Rensselaer County Historical Society when Dr. Albert Corey was State Historian.*
—E. Helen Gardner, 92, retired librarian and teacher, East Greenbush (NY) School District. She also sings alto in the First Church in Albany choir, describing herself as the "eldest chirper."

Larry Staats and I became friends in the 3rd grade. I spent many overnights at Hoogebergh, sometimes for five and six days at a stretch. We sometimes fished in the Hudson for a day's supper. His sister, Janey, and I fell in love and a good part of our courtship took place at the Island. In 1944, wartime, we had our wedding reception and honeymoon there. I'll never forget how Janey's mother, Esther, became more tolerant of our behavior after we all returned from World War II.
—Hans Dirzuweit, 86, retired chemical engineer, F.C. Huyck Company

Children rarely listen—really listen—when the old folks tell tales of history. Vaguely I do remember my mother saying something about a house on an island in the Hudson River and some tie to her ancestors. Imagine my surprise when in 1965 I found myself working with Bill Staats and he invited me to his family homestead, which turned out to be "the house on the island."
—Susanne Stark, retired accounting professor and administrator, Hudson Valley Community College

Hoogebergh provides a secure sense of attachment to my past, present, and future.
—Jennifer Staats Hoeffner, secretary school aide, receptionist

The homestead meant lifelong meaningful memories and relationships, thanks to the Staats family.
—Bob Hart, retired telephone repairman, residing at North Port, Florida

Hoogebergh in winter as sketched by Myrtle Thomas, circa 1982.

LIST OF "RECOLLECTIONS" CONTRIBUTORS

Amrod, James
Benkly, George
Burns, Jim and Jean
Call, Ray
Dirzuweit, Hans
Dyall, James
Erby, Matthew
Fallon, Gretchen and Marty
Fallon, Katie
Gardner, E. Helen
Gubitz, Evelyn
Hart, Bob
Hartnagel, Paul
Hoeffner, Jennifer Staats
Hoeffner, Zachary
Hoey, Leah
Hogg, Thomas
Hutchinson, Fed and Peg
Johnston, Douglas
Kiefer, Patty and Dennis LaPlante, Edward
Lout, Howard
Lucas, Kim Staats
Mast, Rev. Gregg
McCann, Mary Kay
Ming, Audrey
Poulos, Dennis and Betty Jane
Prior, Shirley Snyder
Reimann, William
Shannon, Elizabeth Snyder
Staats, Ethan
Staats, Grant
Stark, Darrell

Stark, Susanne
Stowell, Benjamin
Sweetman, Linda and Ed
Thompson, Dan
VanDyke, Kathy
Velie, Helen Cashman
Williams, Etheleen
Willis, Tientje

Additional copies may be ordered by contacting:

W. L. Staats
9 Stirrup Drive
East Greenbush, NY 12061

Phone (518) 477-5765
E Mail Hoogebergh@aol.com
Website www.onedutchhouse.com

OR

Jennifer Hoeffner
5 Janine Drive
East Greenbush, NY 12061

Phone 518-477-6025
E Mail Jenn8910@verizon.net

37247043R00085

Made in the USA
Lexington, KY
23 November 2014